Re-thinking Social Research

Anti-discriminatory approaches in research methodology

Edited by
BETH HUMPHRIES
CAROLE TRUMAN
Department of Applied Community Studies
Manchester Metropolitan University

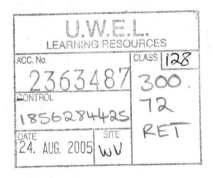
Avebury
Aldershot · Brookfield USA · Hong Kong · Singapore · Sydney

Published by
Avebury
Ashgate Publishing Limited
Gower House
Croft Road
Aldershot
Hants GU11 3HR
England

Ashgate Publishing Company
Old Post Road
Brookfield
Vermont 05036
USA

Reprinted 1996, 1997
Paperback edition 1996

British Library Cataloguing in Publication Data
Re-thinking Social Research:
    Anti-discriminatory Approaches in
    Research Methodology
    I. Humphries, Beth II. Truman, Carole
    300.72

Library of Congress Cataloging-in-Publication Data
Re-thinking social research: anti-discriminatory approaches in
    research methodology / edited by Beth Humphries, Carole Truman.
        p.cm
    Includes index
    ISBN 1-85628-422-5: $58.95 (est:U.S.)
    1. Social policy--Research--Methodology. 2. Social service
    -Research--Methodology. 3. Discrimination. I. Humphires, Beth,
    1940-- II. Truman, Carole, 1960--
    HN29.R36   1994
    300'72--dc20   94-10773
                                                     CIP
ISBN   1 85628 442 5
       1 85972 463 9 (paperback)

Typeset by Tom Tomlinson, 48 Kingsway
Worsley, Manchester, M28 4FD

Printed and bound in Great Britain by
Athenaeum Press Ltd, Gateshead, Tyne & Wear.

Contents

v

Figures and diagrams

Contributors

Ravinder Barn is a Lecturer in Applied Social Studies in the Department of Social Policy and Social Science, Royal Holloway College, University of London. She taught at Middlesex Polytechnic before joining Royal Holloway in 1990. Dr Barn is the author of *Black Children in the Public Care System,* published by Batsford.

Stephen Beyer is Deputy Director of the Welsh Centre on Learning Disabilities, University of Wales, College of Medicine in Cardiff. He has carried out extensive research in the areas of day services and employment for people with learning disabilities as well as research on the contributions of training and quality assurance to organisational change.

Bob Broad is Development Manager with the Royal Philanthropic Society, a voluntary organisation based in Kent helping young people at risk in London and the South East. He has been a probation officer and a social work lecturer at the London School of Economics and the University of Westminster. He is currently an academic examiner, as well as a CCETSW external assessor to a DIPSW programme.

Derek Clifford now teaches social work at Liverpool John Moores University. Previously, whilst involved in parenting two children, he was a childcare social worker, having qualified in 1979. Prior to this, he lectured in political theory in Australia and the West Indies, completing his doctorate in 1972.

Beth Humphries has worked in the social work statutory and voluntary sector, and has carried out research in a number of areas including professional ideologies, women and computer assisted learning. She completed her doctorate in 1983 and since has been teaching in higher education. She is currently head of social work at The Manchester Metropolitan University.

Lynn Keenaghan graduated as a mature student following extensive employment experience with a number of voluntary agencies in the Midlands. After graduation she worked as a freelance HIV trainer and researcher. She is author of *'Voluntary Contributions?'*, a report on the potential for voluntary sector HIV provision in Macclesfield district (1993), distributed by the Health Promotion Unit, Macclesfield. She is currently research and development officer for a social services policy development unit in Oldham.

Marion Martin has worked in nursing, social work and higher education. She has a special interest in community education working within a people-centred philosophy. In addition to her UK experience she has worked in community health in rural South India and Tanzania. She is currently a lecturer in Education for Primary Health Care at the University of Manchester.

Kathleen Pitcairn studied for a BA in Sociology and then a MSc in Social Research Methods at Teesside Polytechnic whilst working in an Adult Training Centre. Later, employed as a Research Associate on a project conducted by the University of Newcastle upon Tyne, she helped to evaluate schemes of care in the community for people with a learning disability.

Mary Scally is a lecturer in the Centre for Applied Social Studies, Swansea University. She has played a prominent role in the field of community development in Ireland. Since 1985 she has been engaged in research in Wales on unemployment and poverty, and more recently on the contribution of training to organisational change.

Carole Truman is senior lecturer in the Department of Applied Community Studies at The Manchester Metropolitan University where she teaches methods of social research at undergraduate and postgraduate level. She has undertaken research in the areas of Equal Opportunities, Women and 'Work'. She is currently Principal Investigator in a project evaluating the planning and provision of services to elderly people.

Preface

Social research has applications in academic settings and in the planning and evaluation of services to the public, private and voluntary sectors. This book is for those in academic institutions and in the welfare professions who have been seeking to explore the theoretical and practical possibilities of anti-discriminatory research. It is an attempt to provide an opportunity to consider where we have come to in attempts to make perspectives of oppressed groups central to the research process.

Originally we had hoped to explore these issues in a conference setting, but for a number of reasons the conference did not take place. The interest that was generated to the idea of a conference in anti-discriminatory research was sufficient to bring together a number of researchers who wanted to share their experiences of doing research within a broad anti-discriminatory framework. There are not many spaces for critical social research with respect to sexism, racism, poverty, sexuality, disability, inequality, and those who have contributed to this volume show a fair degree of courage in defying such a climate to make alternative voices heard. We are grateful to all our contributors, not just for the chapters they have written but for the implicit support they have given to this project along the way.

The volume has been constructed in a political climate which is not encouraging to an examination of issues of inequality. Indeed a preoccupation with 'isms' and 'ologies' is under attack by for example Alastair Law in the Sunday Express, 11.4.93 and Brian Appleyard in the Independent 4.8.93. Hostile articles such as these in national newspapers are indicative of the backlash against any attempt to tackle inequality. Yasmin Alibhai-Brown describes this as 'McCarthyism to counteract imagined totalitarianism' (Independent 11.8.93).

Fear of the 'politically correct' label has spread among researchers, lecturers and professionals, and the pressure now is to bend over backwards to be seen to offer 'balance'.

A major motivation in bringing together this collection was to demonstrate that such research is still going on, and to make available its potential. We hope that other researchers will be encouraged in their choices of topic and methods, to contribute to debates which determine social policies and priorities in a context of deepening inequality, poverty and social exclusion.

Whilst hoping to inform and to encourage researchers in this field we know of several whose contribution to this book we have very much desired, but who as a result of a number of factors were unable to produce their chapters on time. Some of them are members of minority groups under pressure to 'perform' in a number of sometimes competing arenas and who in the end find themselves having to set priorities. We hope their contributions will find expression in other volumes and look forward to a wide circulation of future additions to explicitly anti-discriminatory research.

Finally we would like to acknowledge and thank a number of colleagues who in their various ways have given us support to produce this book. In particular, in the Department of Applied Community Studies of Manchester Metropolitan University, Malcolm Payne provided different pockets of funding along the way and David Boulton undertook the task of indexing. Tom Tomlinson patiently wrestled with different word-processing packages to produce the camera-ready copy. We are also grateful to Avebury for bringing this volume to press.

Beth Humphries

Carole Truman

Department of Applied Community Studies
The Manchester Metropolitan University

1 Re-thinking social research: Research in an unequal world

Carole Truman and Beth Humphries

Like most books on the topic of social research, this volume aims to explore issues in the research process which assist in doing 'better' research in order to achieve an improved understanding of the social worlds in which we live. For us however, 'better' research does not mean the production of 'better' definitive data through improved techniques. It implies a new framework of political will to confront inequalities in the research process and in wider society, and to be politically committed to contributing to social change. The need for rigor is no less important - indeed we would argue that traditional research approaches employ only a partial view of social issues. Our aim in compiling this volume has been to abandon that partial view, whilst at the same time achieving a conscious partiality with those who are marginalised or invisible, or whose experiences have been distorted by traditional research.

This chapter sets out to offer an overview of the problems raised in the conceptualisation and implementation of much mainstream research, which tends to perpetuate rather than challenge social divisions by accepting taken-for-granted premises about social relationships. The chapter goes on to examine alternative approaches, identifying risks and weaknesses and exploring dimensions of an anti-discriminatory approach. It concludes by offering a summary of the structure of the book.

The starting point of the book is how the diversity of experience within the society can be explored through the research process in ways that recognise and value difference. Traditional means of stratifying society only on the basis of class have proved to be deficient in providing representations and explanations of social divisions. Social movements such as the women's movement, black civil rights groups, alliances of people with disabilities and lesbian and gay rights groups have all pointed to the need to broaden (and to change) our understanding of what we mean when we talk about 'society'. Whilst remaining consistent with the theme of diversity, a major focus for this book is on how the research process can confront 'difference' in a positive way, and on how 'difference' impacts on the process of social research. Our approach is concerned less with the mechanics of research methods and more with the underlying assumptions which inform different aspects of the research process. The various authors address this in a number of ways which explore both the processes and topics of research which exist within an anti-discriminatory research framework.

Theoretical debates and practicalities are brought together through an examination of the *processes* of conducting research. We have aimed to offer a collection of papers which in their different ways revert to first principles. Each paper explores how assumptions are too easily built into research studies which contribute to the experiences of marginalised groups being distorted, misrepresented or ignored. Our contributors show how the process of research needs to make assumptions explicit, and how this needs to continue through every stage of a study, so that the conceptual basis for categories used throughout the research become as much a part of the research process as the aims and objectives of the research itself.

A second objective which we pursue is to explore how the topics chosen for examination in conventional research are usually dictated by political interests of researchers or funders' priorities. Again, these priorities which inevitably also constitute constraints on the research process, are rarely problematised when research is written up and disseminated. The problem of research that is left 'undone' for example, is one aired in the chapter by Truman. Problems arising from unclear or conflicting priorities among funders and researchers are discussed in the chapter by Scally and Beyer. These contributions like the others in the book, were chosen because of their focus on issues of oppression and inequality, and their attempts to make visible the particular concerns affecting marginalised groups, as well as the often unspoken pressures on researchers in investigating topics which have been confined to the margins.

Conceptual and methodological imperialism

The process of conceptualising issues so that they can be topics for social research is the cornerstone of all research, whether it is theoretical or empirical. Smith (1987) refers to the persistence of conceptual imperialism which has characterised social relations within social research, where the boundaries of inquiry are set within the framework of what is already established. She refers to the traditions within sociology that organise from a determinate position in society which is 'a ruling class, white male one' (Smith 1987:84). For Smith the outcome of this conceptual imperialism is 'to impose the concepts and terms in which the world of men is thought as the concepts and terms in which women must think their world' (Smith 1987:86). Martin in this volume takes as one of her topics the 'cultural invasion' inherent in much research, leading to a process of 'anti-dialogue' in the research process. Other writers have pointed out that this conceptual imperialism is not just based in a male power position, but that it is also white, eurocentric, heterosexual and able-bodied (Ahmad and Sheldon 1993, Oliver 1992, Stanfield and Dennis, 1993).

Take for example the use of personal characteristics as a means of classification. The task of categorising people is a common element within the social research process. Studies of different forms of inequality need to differentiate for instance the experiences of black people from the experiences of white people, or the experiences of disabled people from those of non-disabled people. However it is neither the *blackness* or *whiteness*, nor the *disability* or *non-disability* that forms the focus of the investigation, but the differential *experiences* of being black or white, or being disabled or non-disabled that fundamentally reveal how inequalities are maintained. Graham points out that

> most typologies do not invite people to record their experiences of racism, but to define themselves in terms of physical and cultural attributes...'race' typologies typically combine a complex of dimensions into a single scale (Graham 1993:32)

In the case of categories on race, a single scale may use political boundaries (Indian, Pakistani, Bangladeshi), geographical definitions (African, European) and colour (black, white) as a means of differentiating one group of people from another. Thus some individuals are asked to define themselves according to their colour whilst others are given different criteria with which to identify. Where only a single choice is permitted, any 'otherness' of a person's identity remains hidden, and indeed is refused. On these scales, someone who is 'black' would be unable to identify as also 'European'. Ahmad and Sheldon (1993) criticise this 'culturalist, geographical and 'nationalist' notion of 'race' dressed up as ethnicity'. Sivanandan (1991) argues that such categorisation plays into the hands of racists by creating and consolidating 'ethnic' differences, fragmenting the oppressed, separating not only 'us' from 'them', but also different sorts of 'them'. The result is a racialization and stereotyping of the very groups which the data purport to support.

The categorisation of individuals by personal characteristics is not a neutral exercise and has consequences which go beyond simple inclusion, exclusion or misrepresentation of certain groups. There has been considerable debate on the appropriateness of categorising data along the lines of 'race' or ethnicity (Anwar 1990; Bhrolchain 1990; Leech 1989). Ahmad and Sheldon set out their concerns about the collection of 'race' statistics:

> Proponents of collecting 'ethnic data' often proceed as if no useful information on 'ethnicity' were available, and by implication that the only barrier to the eradication of racial discrimination is the lack of ethnic data. It is doubtful if social policy would be hampered by the exclusion of the 'ethnic question' in the Census (Ahmad and Sheldon 1993:124)

Bob Broad in this volume, as well as discussing these issues, goes on to examine the controversies surrounding the political definition of the term 'black', which includes people both of African and Asian origin, adopted to emphasise a common experience of and a determination to resist experiences of racism. Its use was also intended to undermine attempts to misuse ethnic data. On the other hand it has been argued that this political definition has been imposed upon certain groups, usually without their consent. Broad predicts that the debates surrounding the topic will 'run and run'.

Barn, also in this volume provides an excellent example of the need to move away from categories of personal characteristics and to focus instead upon the social relations that underpin the area of investigation. She argues that all too often black children appear in social research only when they are the interrogative focus of 'a problem'. She is supported in this by Booth (1988) who points out how in Britain the collection of data on 'race' and ethnicity has been carried out alongside concerns about the 'race problem', and how these statistics have contributed to evidence used to justify racist immigration laws and anti-black feeling. Booth identifies the main issues resting not with definitive data but a new framework of political will aimed at reducing and eradicating racial disadvantage and discrimination.

The usefulness of 'ethnic data' is limited unless it is defined specifically in relation to the purpose of the study: 'to improve the acceptability of hospital food, the hospital should enquire about food habits; religion and the regional background may be useful proxy variables for this - being an 'Indian' clearly is not' (Ahmad and Sheldon 1993:129).

The issues raised by Barn, Booth and Ahmad and Sheldon illustrate how little attention has been paid to systems that allow the dominant ideology to problematise black people. Barn's contribution to this volume provides a detailed examination of how such systems operate within social services departments. The focus of her research then shifts towards exposing the limitations within the system rather than constructing the child as the 'problem'.

Hilary Graham (1993) highlights further problems in the use of categorisation in mainstream research. Surveys such as the General Household Survey (GHS) use a classification system based on an individual's legal status in terms of whether they are 'Married', 'Cohabiting', 'Single', 'Widowed', 'Divorced' or 'Separated'. This classification system fails to represent the meanings that individuals give to their personal relationships. Many domestic relationships and sexual relationships are excluded from this system of classification. There is no category to describe the situation of people living in shared or communal houses. An individual may be 'separated' and also 'cohabiting' with someone on a temporary basis. Within the GHS the definition of 'cohabitation' can only be used in heterosexual relationships. As Graham points out, two friends, two sisters, or people in lesbian or gay relationships cannot, in the GHS 'cohabit'. It is only their place outside the legal institution of 'marriage' that can be recorded. Consequently the GHS and other surveys which use a similar classification system, provide a distorted view of the range of social relations that exist because of the centrality of 'marriage' in the range of definitions.

In this volume, Keenaghan relates the consequences for those engaged in lesbian and gay research of redressing the invisibility of lesbians and gay men in everyday life. Keenaghan goes beyond using research to make visible what has previously been invisible. Lesbians do not necessarily become visible when they conduct research since the same social relationships which make lesbians and gay men invisible are intrinsically contained *within* the research process itself.

Categorisations are useful in social research only where they help us to improve our understanding of the social relationships and experiences that we are trying to explore. Fixed and pre-defined systems of classification that are simply 'bolted-on' to the end of questionnaires, or added as the final set of issues in qualitative research may only redress the problem of 'invisibility' by replacing it with the problems of distortion or misrepresentation. Returning to the example of the General Household Survey, a question was asked whereby individuals are required to classify their personal relationships in the context of the household where they live. The information which the survey elicits in reality is about how individuals define themselves relative to the legal institution of marriage. The survey is problematic for the groups of people who do not fit into the categories that are provided, but is also problematic for the instigators of the survey. By asking a question about personal relationships in such a narrowly defined way, they fail adequately to conceptualise the issue that they are trying to explore. The data they gather not only excludes certain groups of people, it also misrepresents the people who are included in the survey. The labels 'co-habiting' and 'married' do not necessarily tell us very much about the personal relationships of heterosexual people who are living together. As Graham points out:

> Women in husband-absent marriages are classed as married, while they like many lone mothers take sole responsibility for the home and the children (Graham 1993:34)

A more appropriate form of question would challenge the usefulness of the concept of 'marriage' as a way of exploring types of personal relationships. Researchers need to re-think how information is to be used to reach an understanding, and how categories can help to enhance that understanding. It should be the aims and objectives of the research process that influence the operationalisation of concepts and the choice of categories used. If categories fail to improve our understanding of the issues under investigation, they fail to contribute to the research process and need to be returned to the drawing board.

Classifications of disability are another example of how a 'label' can distort the social realities of what being disabled can mean. The effects of disability are not fixed or constant. The experience of disability can vary from one individual to another and can change from one context to another. As many disabled people have highlighted, it is the social and physical environments in which we live rather than an individual's physical condition which construct the consequences of disability (Morris 1990, 1991). Simply adding a question on 'disability' will not make the experiences of disabled people visible in the products of social research, unless the remainder of the research process is designed in such a way as to pick up the breadth of conditions that may be experienced by disabled and non-disabled people. Pitcairn in this volume exposes the inadequacies of research which fails to address itself to the realities of people with learning disabilities. Like other contributors she demonstrates how a fundamental re-thinking of the research process and of the social relationships within it is needed in order to provide an insight into the lives and experiences of people with learning disabilities.

Finally we want to draw attention to the issue of how such problems of classification as we have identified above lead to problems in interpretation and use of data. Macourt (1994) provides a useful discussion of this in a paper on the meanings of information given in the 1991 Northern Ireland Census about 'religion, religious denomination or Body' to which a person belongs (a question not included in the Census in England and Wales). On the face of it data emerging from this question could be expected to be of use in examining differences in say, unemployment to explore hypotheses about structural inequality in Northern Ireland society, characterised by Macourt as 'tribal analysis'. The data could also be used to predict 'when 'they'/'we' will take over' (a reference to the belief that the Catholics will predominate numerically sooner or later), what Macourt calls 'tribal prediction' (p13). Macourt identifies a number of questions related to the interpretation and use of 'tribal analysis'. Some of these are to do with the issues of classification and of non-response (the question is explicitly non-mandatory, and in the 1991 Census there were according to Macourt around 200,000 people for whom no instant classification by 'tribe' can be instantly made), but also the widespread *belief* that a substantial majority of people in Northern Ireland identify with one or the other of the two socio-political-'tribal' groups, Protestant-Unionist and Catholic-Nationalist. Macourt cites evidence to show that such data has been used as a major source in 'tribal analysis', and raises the question as to whether it *ought to be* and *on what basis*. Furthermore Macourt says that 'tribal predictions' have been made ever since Northern Ireland became a separate jurisdiction and even before:

Since the link between religious affiliation and constitutional preference was regarded - for all practical purposes - as complete, the decision taken 75 years ago on which counties should be included in a separate jurisdiction, was based on an interpretation of the results from the 1911 Census. The detailed findings... of the religious question in that Census formed the raw material upon which the ill-fated Boundary Commission of 1924 based its recommendations (Macourt 1994:15)·

Questions Macourt leaves us with, concern the *need* for certain sorts of data, the *uses* to which it has and can be put and the *meanings* attached both to the

7

question as posed and to the answers received. His review of attempts to find answers to the 'religious denomination question' over the past hundred years leads to the conclusion that the political interpretation and the uses to which the Census has been put may have made no small contribution to current conflicts. It is still possible to publicise the conclusion from an analysis of the 1991 Census data that less than half of the population of Northern Ireland declared themselves as belonging to a non Roman Catholic Christian denomination. To what purpose?

These examples show how conceptual imperialism leads to methodological imperialism and to use for political purposes. The categories and sets of procedures which are seen to be 'appropriate' for the collection of data are grounded in the same assumptions which led to the formulation of the research questions, and indeed which led to the social conditions under investigation. They are not called into question and their 'taken-for-grantedness' determines what is observed, what is reported and what action is implemented.

Critique-based alternatives

This broader definition of conceptual and methodological imperialism has profound implications for any research that goes beyond or which challenges dominant ideology. The most obvious starting point for alternative perspectives is to provide a critique of dominant ideology. One of the functions of developing a critique is to map out alternative perspectives on a research topic, or to chart new areas for research. This may be achieved if the researcher re-orientates the focus of the research in a way that makes the new perspective more central. However the more central the alternative perspective becomes the greater the danger of developing an essentialist approach within the research process[1]. An example of how this move towards essentialism can occur may be seen in some of the work of feminists who seek to 'uncover' women's lives within a 'male' world, and thus begin to critique male knowledge. The problem with such analyses is that they are self-referential in their understandings, assuming a common oppression of women regardless of geographical, cultural and ethnic and other boundaries. As hooks (1981) and Lorde (1984) for example have pointed out, these critiques provide only a limited (and therefore distorted) analysis, and fail to take account of the diversity of women's experience. Moreover the whole status of 'experience' as the ground (and the most stable ground) for knowledge production has been called into question with the advent of poststructuralist thought, which has placed it convincingly 'under erasure' (see for example Fuss 1989). Judith Butler makes the point that the political assumption that there must be a universal basis for feminism, one which must be found in an identity assumed to exist cross-culturally, often accompanies the notion that the oppression of women has some singular form discernable in the hegemonic structure of patriarchy. She asserts that:

...gender is not always constituted coherently or consistently in different historical contexts ...gender intersects with racial, class, ethnic, sexual and regional modalities of discursively constituted identities. As a result, it becomes impossible to separate out 'gender' from the political and cultural intersections in which it is invariably produced and maintained (Butler 1990, p3)

In this volume, Humphries discusses some of the consequences of essentialist assumptions in the research process, and the opposition to it which has come from Third World women in particular. Essentialist critiques of oppressive structures and their impact on women, have paved the way for an alternative imperialism based on the very structures of power through which emancipation is sought. Such critiques fail in the attempt to hold on to the notion of women as a group without submitting to the idea that it is a common 'nature' which categorises them as such.

A further problem with critique-based alternatives is that they have to begin with an acknowledgement of the dominant ideological conceptualisation as a means of providing a basis for the critique. However the reverse is not true in as much as writers from the dominant perspective can all too easily continue to write about the world as though alternative perspectives do not exist. The problem is compounded if competing perspectives get 'added in' to the dominant research model. The picture quickly becomes complex and clouded as each new perspective is welded on to the dominant model. What remains intact, albeit well hidden, is the basic framework of the dominant model which, under the weight of numerous critiques continues to operate as a frame of reference.

The search for alternatives

If a critique-based approach ultimately provides few ways forward, what other alternatives are there? Part of the problem which we are trying to overcome is the marginalisation that takes place when researchers attempt to provide

9

alternative perspectives to dominant ideology. Having described part of the process of how this marginalisation occurs, the next task is to explore alternative ways of creating an approach to research which does not rely on a critique of the dominant model. In this section, we will explore two approaches which in their different ways go to the very heart of the dominant models: the reconceptualisation of heterosexuality (Wilkinson and Kitzinger 1993), and the study of men and masculinities (Hearn and Morgan 1990).

The first example we use is Wilkinson and Kitzinger's (1993) work where a marginal position has been used to challenge and reconstruct the central components of a dominant ideology. In response to being asked to produce a 'lesbian special' edition of a journal, Wilkinson and Kitzinger argue that rather than their producing explicitly lesbian perspectives as an alternative to heterosexuality, there is much work that needs to be done by heterosexuals themselves to explicitly conceptualise and explore heterosexuality. Too often they argue, heterosexuality has been taken for granted unless overt alternatives are put forward. Yet the central model of heterosexuality remains under-theorised by heterosexuals:

> In both feminism and psychology, heterosexuality disappears into the background, leaving lesbianism as the interrogative focus [...] we foreground heterosexuality as requiring analytic attention (Kitzinger and Wilkinson 1993:1)

To redress the imbalance, Wilkinson and Kitzinger invited heterosexual feminists to provide written accounts of their heterosexuality. The issues they raised were based upon questions that were often used to explore the topic of lesbianism. There were several areas of focus including: 'What is heterosexuality, and why is it so common?'; 'How does heterosexuality affect the whole of a woman's life?'. Only one question was addressed to how heterosexuality might contribute to feminist politics. A variety of responses was received, but the majority were unable to engage in the political implications of their heterosexuality outside the private parameters of particular heterosexual relationships. There is a dearth of analysis addressing ' the way that heterosexuality operates as an institution vis-a-vis unemployment, the law, social services, the economy, education...isn't there a pressing need to understand how heterosexuality functions in relation to unemployment, poverty, homelessness?' (Swindells 1993:41).

10

The editors reported their 'delight' at the 'recognition of the implicit politics which inspires the reversal of all those Special Issues on lesbians (p1). Yet as Swindells comments, the range of responses that were elicited did very little to explore the way that formations operate 'between men and women throughout the public and social world' (1993:42). Theorising heterosexuality is an important challenge to our understanding of social relations, but it is a challenge that still remains to be met.

The second example we use is the growing literature on 'men and masculinities' (see for example Chapman and Rutherford 1988, Hearn 1987), which has emerged to re-examine the nature of 'men' as a response to work done by feminists. One of the underlying themes in this body of literature is that feminists have argued that knowledge which claims to be about 'people' is really about men. One of the responses of feminists has been to redress the balance by focusing on doing research which is explicitly about women. The concerns of the 'men and masculinities' literature is that if research that claims to be about people is actually about men, then there is a problem not just for women, but also for men. If men are subsumed within the category 'people', then the uniqueness of the category 'man' is lost. The consequence of this is that 'ungendered' research ignores the experiences of women, but distorts the experiences of men. Thus 'ungendered' research has only limited applicability to the lives of men.

In contrast to the emerging debate on heterosexuality, the study of men has taken place within a broad political arena. Contained within its literature are accounts of 'work', unemployment, pornography, politics and power. Nevertheless there remain considerable weaknesses and shortcomings within the discourse.

Morgan (1992) provides a lengthy discussion on 'work' and picks up many themes that have emerged in feminist literature. He then explores some of the implications for men that appear in feminists accounts of 'work'. Morgan unquestioningly uses a very narrow definition of work in his discussion - that of paid work in the public sphere. In so doing he fails to explore some of the major feminist insights to the study of work, in particular that paid work exists in both the public and private spheres, and that many of the issues around women's paid work can only be understood within the context of their unpaid work. Similarly, there is no attention given to the paid work that is done outside the formal workplace.

One of the problems with the study of men lies in the arena in which much of the discussion takes place. As Jalna Hanmer points out, the roots of the study of men rest largely as a response to the political and academic work of feminists.

11

This provides a contrast to the origins of feminist scholarship which are with the women's movement and social and political change for women (see also Truman in this volume). The work of feminists is present both inside and outside academic life. However, Hanmer argues that the study of men lacks the same political roots of making women visible, and too often fails to acknowledge, recognise or cite contributions from feminist scholars. 'In practice this means that women scholars have to read both what women and men write while scholarly men continue to need to read only each other' (Hanmer 1990:24).

A large contribution to the feminist literature has been around epistemology and methodology. Feminists have taken pains to explore methodologies which are consistent with different forms of feminist investigation (Fonow and Cook 1991; Harding 1987; Roberts 1981; Stanley 1990). So far, the study of men has not developed the same concerns with epistemological and methodological issues.

Both of the above approaches provide an interesting departure from work that is based on providing 'alternative perspectives' on dominant ideology. The question is, can this 're-conceptualisation' approach provide a useful basis for doing research? Part of the problem with both approaches is that availability of empirical data is scarce. They exist primarily as theoretical discussions and thus provide few clues about how they might impact upon the process of empirical research. The critical test of re-defining research problems will be, if in practice our understanding is improved of the social relations involved. For studies of men, a critical issue will be whether men can tell us anything about themselves and the power relations to which they contribute, that feminists have not told us already. The test for theories of heterosexuality will be if they can progress beyond personal descriptive accounts of sexual relationships, and develop frameworks which use political analyses of heterosexuality. These seem to be tasks for men and women as well as for gay and straight, so that the arguments can move on rather than remaining static or being shelved as an issue that 'has been done'.

The discussion above represents a potentially de-colonising move by re-defining the research 'problem' at both conceptual and methodological levels. Although we are critical of some aspects of these approaches, the principle of re-definition is an important part of the process of re-formulating dominant ideology. Clifford in this volume attempts to construct a model for researching critical life courses by questioning assumptions at every stage, and adopting an approach which incorporates biographical, historical, sociological factors, underpinned by a concern to pursue research in the light of social and historically specific relations of power and dominance.

The process of re-definition also contains what Ladner (1987) calls a 'critical disclosure' - the insight that research does not constitute an 'objective' knowledge, but is a constructed reality. Ladner describes her experience of having been equipped in her academic training with a deviant perspective of black communities, and the expectation that her research with young black women would be to 'validate and elaborate on what was alleged to exist' (p75). However as a black woman she found it impossible to play the role of the impartial social scientist, 'because all of my life experiences invalidated the deviant perspective' (p76). She argues that the basic concepts and tools of white Western society are permeated by a partiality to the 'conceptual framework of the oppressor'. Ladner increasingly became aware that she brought to her research the attitudes, values and beliefs, and in effect a Black perspective, that were central to her own identity. This led her to abandon the deficit model of black communities, and to describe 'their power to cope and adapt to a set of unhealthy conditions - not as stereotyped sick people but as normal ones' (p96). This provided the conditions for an alternative way of thinking and an appropriate methodology.

Similar issues arose for Keenaghan as described in her chapter. Given the potential for invisibility as a lesbian researcher however, her discussion about censorship and self-censorship, and the questions she raises as to who benefits and who loses out as a result of such censorship, is a crucial added dimension to debates about 'objectivity' and the impact of self-disclosure.

It has been argued elsewhere that such an alternative approach is underpinned by ethical concerns (for example May 1993). We are critical of the discussions about ethics which we find in the literature on research methods, and some analysis of this dimension is necessary before we proceed to examine anti-discriminatory alternatives.

The 'ethical' red herring

Most textbooks on methods include some discussion of ethical concerns within the research process. However the way in which 'ethics' has been conceptualised varies considerably. The majority of discussions on ethics is concerned with the rights of research subjects (see for example BSA 1991). Thus for research to be ethical it should be informed by moral principles which avoid

13

harming others, which promote the good and which are respectful and fair (Seiber 1993). Where codes of practice exist, they are voluntary (eg. American Sociological Association Voluntary Code of Practice). They are premised on 'professional' norms, but with no penalties for breach of ethics. In reality, where discussion of ethics appears, it consists of the researcher *justifying* her/his ethical behaviour, and we know of no account of ethics where the researcher admits to unethical practice. There is therefore no positive benefit to discussions of ethics, since there are no measures of poor practice and no penalties for breach. The consequences for research subjects are that they are dependent on the goodwill of researchers whether or not an ethical code exists or is applied.

A fundamental problem with discussions about ethics is that because they are framed within sanitised 'professional ideals' they do not grasp the nettle of power and politics which are inherent in the research process. The context in which research is conducted, the social characteristics of researched and researcher, methods, strategies, conclusions all result in power and control of the research by the researcher. It could be argued that 'ethics' and 'politics' are inseparable, yet the use of 'political' injects elements of controversy into the research equation and is all too often used by opponents to stigmatise views and perspectives. This volume is being produced in a climate which is not encouraging to an examination of issues of inequality.

For the reasons we have set out here, although ethical and political concerns underpin the objectives of this volume, they do not provide a useful framework because of the inadequacies of the debates surrounding them, and because of the defensive stance which characterises the theoretical conceptualisation of ethics. We must search for terminology which offers a framework for positive assessment of how research is conceived and carried out.

We have adopted the term 'anti-discriminatory' then, to describe the kind of research the authors in this volume are attempting to pursue. By this we mean not a neutral, detached, 'hands off' concern with 'doing no harm'. We mean rather an active involvement in challenging assumptions based on unequal social relations, through reflexive, explicitly committed participation in the process of social change. Bob Broad's chapter opens with his reasons for choosing 'anti-discrimination' rather than 'equal opportunities', which in his view has come to mean all things to all people. Humphries in her chapter in this volume, warns of the risks of the use of language only towards an accommodation of dominant values. By contrast, the term anti-discriminatory clearly means *against* discrimination, working for change against all forms of discrimination and

14

oppression. Ladner, in describing her struggles with 'objectivity' in research with black women tells us,

'The inability to be objective about analyzing poverty, racism, disease, self-destruction, and the gamut of problems which faced these females only mirrored a broader problem in social research. That is, to what extent should any scientist - white or Black - consider it his(sic) duty to be a dispassionate observer and not intervene, when possible, to ameliorate many of the destructive conditions he studies' (Ladner 1987:79)

The attempt here is to make such intervention as Ladner describes, at every level of the research process, by practising anti-discriminatory research. The question we have arrived at then is, what might be some of the characteristics of an anti-discriminatory alternative?

A key flaw in dominant ideology is that it fails to take on board diversity within its own conceptualisation - the diversity of experience beyond that 'norm' - and so ultimately fails to locate itself within the diversity of social relations. We have made a case for difference and diversity within the social world. Exploring and locating difference must be central to research process. However the exploration of difference does not just constitute a descriptive component of the research process; it also provides a marker for the power relations that generate 'difference'. Unless 'difference' becomes an explicit aspect of research the power relationships within the research process are obscured.

In deciding on research topics, the direction of an anti-discriminatory approach is not necessarily towards 'sensitive' topics - those which are threatening in some way to those who are studied (Renzetti and Lee 1993). Indeed doing research on sensitive topics does not necessarily render them visible. As Truman argues in this volume, adding the 'feminist' label to research on women provides an access point for women, but enables it to be ignored or 'picked off' by anti-feminists. Thus feminist knowledge exists outside of dominant discourse. Topics for research cannot be separated from the structures and processes through which knowledge is constructed and evolves. The wisdoms on sensitive topics seem to exist in a ghetto and the question arises as to whether people researching in the mainstream will have anything to learn. As Kitzinger and Wilkinson conclude, 'Lesbians will become visible within feminism only when the institution of compulsory heterosexuality becomes a serious target for analysis and political action' (1993:12)

15

The direction of anti-discriminatory research is away from 'deviant', pathological perspectives. There must be a strong concern with re-defining the problem:

consider for instance, research on domestic violence. The question that has dominated this area of enquiry for more than two decades has been this: Why do battered women stay with partners who abuse them? Regardless of the answers generated, posing the question itself establishes the parameters of the problem of partner abuse in terms of the behaviour of battered women. Attention is deflected from batterers onto victims. It is battered women who are defined as deviant for remaining in abusive relationships not their partners who are deviant for battering them. In short, asking 'why do battered women stay?' rather than 'what factors make battering possible or even permissable?.....' creates a scientific and popular milieu for blaming the victim.   Renzetti and Lee 1993:28

Similarly instead of searching for clues as to why black people are more vulnerable to schizophrenia than white, a research question might be, 'what are the social processes which lead to a disproportionate number of black people being diagnosed as schizophrenic?' Again, 'in what ways do sexually abused adolescent girls exhibit over-sexualized behaviour?' might be replaced with, 'what factors contribute to the recovery of survivors of sexual abuse?'

But we would not wish to focus only on research topics. The whole process of conducting research is likely to be imbued with discriminatory elements unless steps are taken to confront the inequality which exists. Thus an anti-discriminatory approach spans beyond the choice of topic, or relationships in the field, and provides a framework that is integral to the entire research process. Issues related to the context and orientation of research for instance, are raised in a number of contributions in this volume. Barn describes how the issues surrounding black children in the care system have been of a 'problem oriented nature', with little emphasis on the circumstances surrounding how those children entered the system. Broad upholds the need to contextualise all research and practice as starting within a racist and sexist society. Humphries provides a framework to challenge the discriminatory processes within social research studies.

Taking anti-discriminatory research approaches as the organising theme, the book covers a number of dimensions of the effort towards re-conceptualising research, ranging across theoretical, political and practical concerns. Carole

16

Truman sets the scene by examining the scope of feminist critiques of traditional research and asks, has it gone far enough and what are its limitations? Ravinder Barn confronts the problems and barriers in negotiating research access in her study of black children in care of local authorities. Kathleen Pitcairn describes in detail her methods of interviewing the so-called 'uninterviewable' - people with profound learning disabilities, whilst Lynn Keenaghan explores some of the issues of sexuality and sexual identity raised in her study of levels of knowledge about HIV. Derek Clifford attempts to construct a multi-disciplinary methodology for anti-oppressive critical life history research. Marion Martin's chapter unpacks the detail of a feminist participative approach to research with a women's health project and offers a framework for evaluating the extent to which participation has been achieved. Mary Scally and Steve Beyer have been working for a number of years on the all-Wales Strategy for the Development of Services for Mentally Handicapped People. Their chapter describes how research which aimed to work closely with senior managers met with obstacles which frustrated this intention. Bob Broad's chapter starts with the premise that anti-discriminatory research should be part of a process for promoting social change, and drawing on his experience of the probation service he offers a model to examine tendencies in organisational research towards 'change' and 'no change' anti-discriminatory cycles. Finally Beth Humphries takes a critical look at the notion of 'empowerment' and offers fundamental ingredients for research which makes the claim of 'empowering'.

We have offered little which is original in research methodology. We have not even included entirely innovative areas for research. What we have done is to assemble a collection of papers which individually and collectively have attempted to chip away at the assumptions which are built into research design. We hope that readers will learn from the papers whatever the topic of research and no matter what focus on what topic is taken. By this detailed look at the research process from first principles, we hope to contribute to an on-going movement that will help us all to do 'better' research, to contribute to a better understanding of the social world, and ultimately to change it. Readers will judge for themselves to what extent individual authors and the volume as a whole have achieved this.

Notes

[1] Contemporary debates around the notion of essentialism point up its radical *and* conservative potential, depending on who is utilising it, how it is deployed and where its effects are concentrated. Diana Fuss (1989) herself an anti-essentialist, lays out the terms of the essentialist/constructionist opposition, identifying the political investments and internal contradictions of each. Perhaps a distinction can be made between essentialism as a political strategy and as a theoretical concept. For our purposes here however, it is important to discuss the risks inherent in taken-for-granted assumptions of essentialism in social research.

References

Ahmad WIU and Sheldon TA (1993) 'Race' and Statistics, in ed.
M Hammersley, *Social Research, Philosophy, Politics and Practice*, Sage
Anwar M (1990) 'Ethnic classifications, ethnic monitoring and the 1991
    Census', in *New Community* 16 (4) 606-615
Bhrolchain MN (1990) 'The ethnic question for the 1981 Census: background
    and issues', in *Ethnic and Racial Studies* 13 (4),   543-567
Booth H (1988) 'Identifying ethnic origin: the past, present and future of official
    data production', in A Bhat et al, eds   *Britain's Black Population*, 2nd
    edition, Gower
BSA (1992) 'Statement of ethical guidelines' British Sociological
    Association 1992
Butler J (1990) *Gender Trouble*, Routledge
Chapman R and Rutherford J eds (1988) *Male Order: Unwrapping
    Masculinity*, Lawrence and Wishart
Fonow M and Cook J eds. (1991) *Beyond Methodology: Feminist
    Scholarship as Lived Research*, OUP
Fuss D (1989) *Essentially Speaking*, Routledge
Graham H (1993) *Hardship and Health in Women's Lives*, Harvester
Hanmer J (1990) *Men, Power and the Exploitation of Women*, in J   Hearn and
    D Morgan, eds. op cit.
Harding S ed.(1987) *Feminism and Methodology*, Open University Press/
    Indiana University press
Hearn J (1987) *The Gender of Oppression: Men, Masculinity and the Critique
    of Marxism*, Wheatsheaf
Hearn J and Morgan D eds (1990) *Men, Masculinities and Social Theory*,
    Unwin Hyman
hooks B (1981) *Ain't I a Woman: Black Women and Feminism*, Pluto
Kitzinger C and Wilkinson S (1993) *'Theorising Heterosexuality'* in eds.
    Wilkinson S and Kitzinger C, op cit.
Ladner JA (1987) *Introduction to Tomorrow's Tomorrow: The Black
    Woman*, in ed S Harding, op cit.
Leech K (1989) *A Question in Dispute: The Debate about an 'Ethnic' Question
    in the Census*, London: Runnymede Trust
Lorde A (1984) *Sister Outsider*, The Crossing Press Feminist Series
Macourt M (1994) *Using Census Data: Religion as a Key Variable in Studies of
    Northern Ireland*, in Environment and Planning: A, (forthcoming)

May T (1993) *Social Research: Issues, Methods and Process*, Open University

Morgan D (1992) *Discovering Men*, Routledge

Morris J (1990) *Our Homes, Our Rights: Housing, Independent Living and Physically Disabled People*, London: Shelter

Morris J (1991) *Pride Against Prejudice: transforming attitudes to disability*, Women's Press

Oliver M (1992) Changing the Social Relations of Research Production? in *Disability Handicap and Society*, Vol.7, No.2

Renzetti CM and Lee M eds.(1993) *Researching Sensitive Topics*, Sage

Roberts H (1981) *Doing Feminist Research*, RKP

Seiber J (1993) 'The ethics and politics of sensitive research' in eds CM Renzetti and M Lee, op cit.

Sivanandan A (1991) 'Black struggles against racism', in Curriculum Development Project Steering Group eds. *Setting the Context*, London: CCETSW

Smith D (1987) 'Women's perspective as a radical critique of sociology' in ed S Harding, op cit.

Stanfield JH and Dennis RM eds (1993) *Race and Ethnicity in Research Methods*, Sage

Stanley L ed (1990) *Feminist Praxis: Research, Theory and Epistemology in Feminist Sociology*, Routledge

Swindells J (1993) 'A straight outing' in *Trouble and Strife* 26:40-44

Wilkinson S and Kitzinger C eds (1993) *Heterosexuality: A Feminism and Psychology Reader*, Sage

2 Feminist challenges to traditional research: Have they gone far enough?

Carole Truman

Within the world of social research, there has always broad range of ideologies, conceptual frameworks and methodological approaches which have been practiced, discussed, and debated for more than a century. What all social research has in common, is its claim to provide a better understanding of the social world in which we live and participate. Kuhn (1962) describes how all social research is conducted with reference to other studies, and as such is either implicitly or explicitly, always situated within a paradigm or scientific tradition. A variety of sources provide critiques of the political, epistemological and methodological bases for social research (e.g. Sjoberg, 1967; Shipman, 1988). In ethnography, 'schools' of social research have emerged which have created arenas for debate within a qualitative framework (e.g. Denzin, 1970; Goffman, 1961; McCall and Simmons, 1969). The purpose of this chapter is not to describe or to enter into any of those debates, but to begin to discuss the emergence of feminist research in the late 1970s and early 1980s. Eichler (1988) provides a detailed critique of how sexist assumptions have been built into 'traditional' social research. Thus feminist research began to propose a powerful and radical alternative to 'traditional' (sexist) research practice (Bowles and Duelli Klein, 1983). In contrast to previous debates on and within social research, the emergence of feminist research went beyond a methodological discussion, and demanded a complete re-think of what had been conceptualised as social research.

Feminist research methodology has emerged over the last decade as a challenge to previous wisdoms on what may be considered as research, how research might be conducted and who might be the audiences for social research. There are many factors which differentiate feminist research from other forms and approaches to social research and yet there remains considerable diversity and debate within that which is called feminist methodology. Within the diversity and debate however, there is one consistent strand which unites all perspectives within feminist research: and that is that the roots of feminist scholarship and hence feminist methodology, have always been grounded within a larger women's movement. Through feminist research, the realities of women's lives have begun to be made visible and pressure brought to bear to improve their material and social existence. Yet despite over a decade of active feminist research and debate, much of women's experiences remain marginal and unexplored. Graham describes how in the world of health, women in general, and certain groups of women in particular continue to be mis-represented or un-represented in sources of information on women's lives (1993:16-35). In this chapter I will address some of the implications for women in terms of the contribution that feminist research has made to their lives. I will assess the extent to which it truly provides a re-think of traditional social research in terms of the way it has been able to address the diversity of women's experiences.

One way of describing feminist research is as the bridge between daily reality of women's lives, and the scholarship and analysis which has become Women's Studies and feminism. Today, the voices of popular women's movements are naming diversity and difference in terms of age, disability, class, sexuality, 'race' and ethnicity. The challenge then to feminist research is to explore diversity and difference. The purpose of this chapter is to debate some of the practical and ideological obstacles that exist to feminist research if it is to confront diversity and difference in women's lives. The task then is to describe the process which provides links between the roots of the women's movements and then feeds into feminist debate. Implicit within this task is to explore the scope of feminism as it exists in an international arena in the climate of the 1990s. The question to ask is does the scope of current debate within feminist research have sufficient breadth to bridge the gap?

Feminist research as social research

Although feminists argue that there are characteristics within feminist research which provide it with a distinctiveness from other forms of social research, there is no common definition or understanding of what actually constitutes feminist research. Different authors have discussed a variety of positions within feminist research. For example, early feminist research emphasised the role of a feminist perspective as needing to counteract the male bias which exists in 'conventional' approaches to knowledge and traditional analyses of social life (Roberts, 1981,

22

Oakley, 1981, Smith, 1987, 1988). At this level, research which puts women in the spotlight, or which explores issues from women's perspectives fulfils some of the criteria of that which is called feminist. The consequences of exploring social life from women's position has political consequences, and the very act of being a woman in the arena exposes the realities of the personal being political.

The task of legitimating personal experience as academic knowledge and worthy of academic debate has been and remains no small task (Stanley and Wise, 1983, Stanley, 1990). The 'sexism in sociology' described by Ann Oakley in the early 1970s contributed to a growing body of literature on the disadvantaged position of women on society (Oakley, 1975). Oakley describes the struggle of 'translating into academically - and publicly - acceptable terms a basic perception that housework might be conceived as part of the genus of work, rather than a dimension of femininity' (Oakley, 1984:vii). Early studies of domestic violence faced similar barriers in terms of its acceptability of an area of study and its conceptualisation as an issue. Two decades later, there is still debate about the legitimacy of certain avenues of feminist enquiry within academic scholarship, and many of the conceptual issues that feminists have untangled are all too easily ignored by dominant ideology.

If the topics of feminist enquiry remain open to question, then so too do its methods. Some argue that there are severe limitations in differentiating feminist research from other research literature :

> It [feminist research] is yet another instance of an attempt to set up a separate methodological paradigm based on distinctive political and philosophical assumptions that are held to motivate a unique form of research practice. Like other attempts to do this, it homogenises other research views (Hammersley, 1992:202-3).

It is unusual for debates about feminist methodology to take place anywhere other than within feminist literature. What is interesting (or perhaps predictable) about Hammersley's view is that it engages in the debate only to the extent that arguments on feminist methodology can be dismissed. The accusation that feminism homogenises other research views is useful only as far as it enables a feminist approach to be ignored by non-feminist scholars. Hammersley thus legitimates other researchers to remain oblivious to any contribution that feminists make to dominant (sexist) research literature. The emergence of empirical research that is informed by a feminist analysis, must surely set challenges for all

23

social researchers to contemplate their research practice and research design: if only to explore if it will help them to do better research. Yet arguments are rarely phrased in terms of what feminist research has to offer non-feminists, rather why if feminist perspectives exist what reasons can be found to dismiss them. The culmination of this situation is that feminist debate and scholarship may well illuminate new areas of study and provide new insights on methods, but the main audience for feminist scholarship will be other feminists. We may thus struggle to pioneer new areas of investigation, but we have little control over how our scholarship is absorbed by the academy at large.

The strength of feminist research rests not so much with its position within the Academy, but in relation to the part it plays in the feminist theory. Within this arena, the literature on research methodology is now sufficiently diverse to encompass considerable breadth within feminist methodology.

The boundaries of feminist research

Beyond the scenario described above, Smith states that it is necessary not only to illuminate women's position in society as it is distinct from men's but also to explain why these worlds are separate, how men dominate and what women can do to resist (Smith, 1987). Unless men engage in this enquiry, there is an overwhelming burden for women to come up with the answers. But on these terms it is clear that feminism has much to offer.

In the context of the academy, there is a clear need for feminist research to be presented as something which is distinct from other forms of research. When this happens, there is a danger of creating artificial boundaries within discussions of the research process. The problem however is not as Hammersley suggests, that feminism homogenises other approaches to research, but whether there are problems in trying to achieve internal homogeneity within feminist discussions of research.

The practical basis for feminist research has been to focus on the category of 'woman' as the central concept which differentiates feminist study from other studies. Different writers have commented on the nature of the distinctiveness of feminist research. Harding delineates this distinctiveness by pointing to the problems of simply 'adding' women into dominant analyses of social life. She suggests that the transformation in thinking that would be required to accommodate women's experiences would be too great or may result in women's experiences being subsumed within relativism. The task of using women's experiences as the

24

basis for social analysis is so great that it beckons approaches that are distinct within themselves (Harding, 1987).

A number of themes link that which has become known as feminist research. Fonow and Cook (1991) comment on how many of the features of feminist research reflect the position of feminism within research institutions. The disadvantageous position of women in the social class hierarchy provides a mirror for the position that feminism holds within many academic institutions. Most textbooks take pains to differentiate the distinctiveness of feminist scholarship over other academic approaches. All too often, the outcome of this search for commonality is that differences between women and the diversity of women's lives are understated or blurred.

In the meantime, contemporary women's movements and women's studies have broadened beyond an exploration of commonalities within feminism, to encompass the complexities of issues to do with difference in terms of ethnicity, 'race', social class, disability, age and sexuality. Too often feminism has been accused of failing to address the diversity of women's lives that exists beyond a feminism made from the position of the white, educated, able-bodied. The crux of the problem is not so much to do with issues of methodology, but the breadth of analysis which is used to inform the methods of empirical investigations. Incorporating issues of 'difference' into feminist research requires some basic re-thinking of the research process.

The challenge of difference

Much of the discussion on feminist research sets the parameters so broad that any issue of interest to women, by women is legitimate. When this happens, the outcome is that inequalities which exist within the research process remain hidden. Many authors point to the plurality of women's experiences but this is commonly conceptualised as differences which particular groups of women may bring to different research projects. A simple example of this would be the way feminist research allows black women to bring perspectives on 'race' and culture into the research process, but such perspectives are rarely centralised by white feminists. Thornton Dill describes how the discussion of black womanhood 'first requires rethinking several areas of scholarship about black women and their families' (1987:98). If a category of 'womanhood' is used by all feminists, then all need to engage in this rethinking to re-shape the perspectives brought into feminist enquiry.

The conceptualisation of difference has implications both for theory and for practice. Stanley (1990) sees part of the challenge of difference as locating the feminist researcher firmly within the activities of her research. But in this context difference is described largely in terms of what type of feminist the researcher is, and thus what theoretical or methodological paradigms may influence the production of the research. Here Stanley signals how research may be influenced by different types of feminisms. What is also apparent is that many feminists bring into their research influences which are beyond feminism. The influences outside feminism may well have considerable bearing upon directions for feminist research when exploring issues of difference. In practice, the challenge of difference requires not just a feminist approach which focusses on criteria to do with the notion of 'woman' but also approaches which deal with other aspects of being woman. Locating ones self in the research is not just about declaring marxist or radical influences, but at a more basic level declaring oneself as being white or black, able-bodied or disabled, young or old, inside or outside the academy, and so on. Often these influences are only located within feminist research when the researcher differs from the white, able-bodied, middle-class academic. Just as any feminist research requires new lenses through which to see ourselves, the challenge of doing research which reflects difference between women may actually require new cameras as well.

Conceptualising difference is no small task since it requires a re-thinking of traditional approaches to knowledge and knowledge production. At a theoretical level, academics have been required to address social phenomena which do not fall neatly into discrete academic disciplines, and which certainly test the boundaries of dominant concepts within theory:

> The civil rights and black power movements in the USA, the extensive use of migrant labour, including that from the Third World, in Europe and the growth of contemporary women's movements were all part of the pressure ... to reconceptualise some of the central theoretical ground in order to ... explain the last third of the twentieth century world. (Allen, Anthias and Yuval-Davies, 1991:23)

Difference is a feature of society today, but for academics the need to conceptualise difference has come from outside the walls of the academy and it will long continue to remain the case that the influences of difference will be less within the academy than beyond it. These, and other differences are reflections of the breadth of divisions and inequalities which exist at an individual and social level across the world. At a theoretical level, the variety and consequences of such

26

divisions have been dealt with in very different ways. There is no shortage of theory about certain forms of difference, but there is a paucity of approaches which deal with the inter-connectedness of forms of difference (Brah, 1991). Historically some divisions have been privileged over others and it remains the case that the interrelationship between divisions has remained de-politicised and un-theorised. Allen et al (ibid). point out that the task for theory is to identify how 'different forms of exclusion and subordination operate' (p.24) in different contexts, but moreover how the interconnectedness of such divisions may be transformed into theory. It is thus indicative that the challenge has been set for feminist movement, feminist theory and feminist research to both identify and explore its relationships with other movements and theories based on social divisions.

The task is made more difficult because many differences between women remain under theorised both outside and within feminism. Just one example of this is the way feminism was devalued in the anti-racist struggles of the 1970s whilst at the same time, black perspectives have struggled for their place within feminism (hooks, 1982). Ultimately, feminism needs to encompass notions of difference. Stanley's concept of 'praxis' is a useful way of articulating how it may impact on feminist social research. Through praxis, we may change the world as well as study it, demonstrate the interconnectedness of research and theory and focus explicitly on the 'hows' and 'whats' of research (Stanley, 1991).

Difference and diversity in feminist research

The emergence of contemporary social movements presents a range of challenges for the praxis of feminist social research. Within Women's Studies there is a demand that teaching addresses matters to do with 'race' and culture, disability rights, lesbian issues, the lives of older women and so on. The demands are a result of recognising heterogeneity amongst women and point to the need to confront the diversity of women's experiences. The following part of this paper addresses the competence of the research process to explore and address issues of difference. The framework I use is the the very practical framework of research which incorporates the whys and whats of the research process from design to dissemination. Implicit within this framework is the need to explore the potential of feminist research to learn to listen to different voices (hooks, 1989).

My experience of doing research where women are the central focus comes from ten years of conducting research largely within an academic setting, but where much of the research that I have done has been 'applied' in nature. I believe that issues of difference between women and amongst women present challenges at every point within the research process from the conception of a research idea through to the dissemination of the results. I believe this to be true whether research is conducted within the academy and/or in applied contexts where there may be practical or policy implications.

Feminist epistemology stresses the importance of legitimating research as we personally live it and experience it - thus giving voice to the way that 'the personal is political' underpins feminist research. However where issues of difference and diversity are concerned, the concept of the personal being political may not be enough since it is equally important to draw upon the analysis of others. The nature of our stratified society means that others will experience their lives differently. A personal perspective may be strength within feminist research, but in the context of diversity, it can also be a weakness:

> We must also recognise that our personal experiences are shaped by the culture with all its prejudices. We cannot therefore depend on our perceptions alone as the basis for political analysis and action ... Feminists must stretch beyond, challenging the limits of our own personal experiences by learning from the diversity of women's lives' Bunch, 1988:290

I am not suggesting that feminists have failed to address the practical issues of differences but discussion often privileges particular parts of the research process as being the place where difference has the most impact. For example, Oakley (1981) explores issues of power and difference in the context of the interface between the researcher and the research. In this case, she emphasised the need to diffuse power relations within that part of the research process, by claiming similarities with her research participants. Similarities or differences to do with disability, sexuality 'race' or class characteristics are not mentioned. Gender is seen to be the factor which unites the researcher and the research, and because this is so, differences between the researcher and the researched remain unexplored. This means that any biases in terms of sexuality, disability, 'race' and so on remain unarticulated and therefore invisible within this and other parts of the research process.

Research questions

Almost all the literature on feminist research discusses research which has been done. This may seem obvious, but for every research project which is done there are scores which have been devised which remain undone. Additionally, there will always be research that is left to do. There is intrinsic value within the process of research itself, but this is limited and it is rarely enough just to research. Much of the value of research is around the products of that process and to be seen to be doing that research. For this to happen, research cannot be taken as an isolated act, but an act which at some level needs a constituency and also some sponsorship. Both constituency and sponsorship have their own agendas and biases. For some researchers, it may be the requirement to secure funding to do research, for others it may be that research needs to achieve a level of acceptability - whether to a tutor who is marking it, or a department which will include it in its list of research activities. There is surely no research that has been done where issues of acceptability and sponsorship have not been addressed. Facing these issues demands a degree of personal sponsorship and personal energy. Even at this basic level, the process of difference and hence, inequality within research has begun: there will be some areas of research where funds cannot be found, there will be areas of research where people are not prepared to invest energy, and areas of research where nobody dares.

I had personal experience of this in my own department when a memo was circulated asking for bids for faculty funds. The department where I work is concerned with community issues and for an academic institution, has a strong profile in equal opportunities. Manchester is a lively, modern city and over recent years has amongst other things, become a centre for 'popular culture' with fashion houses and nightclubs. There is a diverse and visible gay community and one part of the city centre is known as the gay village. Against this background, and as a feminist within the department, I put together a proposal to investigate the question: is there a lesbian community in Manchester? I also thought up three other proposals and managed to secure the support of a colleague who put her name on the proposals as well. Of all the proposals, the lesbian community one was the only one that was argued in professional and academic terms and included a bibliography. Our work received promising feedback and we were told to select one proposal to go forward to the faculty. We were told although it was very good and very interesting, we would not choose the lesbian community proposal because 'people would not be interested'.

This vignette raises a number of issues. When I chose to put in a proposal on the lesbian community, I knew it stood no chance of being accepted. However, I felt it important that I did not censor it myself, but force others to make the decision about its acceptability. I therefore invested my energy into putting the proposal together. I also knew that if I did not put in that proposal, it was unlikely that it would get sponsorship from anyone else, even to the first hurdle. However, from my professional perspective, I did not want to be seen to only 'back losers', so I also thought of other 'more acceptable' topics for research. That these were acceptable to other people, gave me licence to be seen as a researcher in the way the lesbian proposal did not. From my point of view, I had to double-think through processes of 'acceptability' and 'unacceptability' both on my terms and on the terms of others in the Department. Sadly, we are a long way from Adrienne Rich's vision of the woman-centred university which might:

> organize its resources around problems specific to its community; for example, adult literacy, public health, safer, cheaper, and simpler birth control; drug addiction; community action; geriatrics ..... most large urban universities have many communities, ... for example not simply black and Puerto Rican, but white middle-class, poor and aged, Jewish, Japanese, Cuban, etc. A sympathetic and concerned relationship with all these groups would involve members of the University in an extremely rich cluster of problems. And the nature of much research would be improved of it were conceived as research for rather than research on human beings' (Rich, 1992:391-2).

There are many stages along the way if we want to redress the diversity of women's experiences. The reality of women's lives suggests a range of constituencies and agendas especially since many women are excluded from the academy, and thus have little or no voice in the research process. The principle applies to all levels of difference and exposes how inequality is bound up with differences. The words of Audre Lorde make the point forcibly:

> It is the members of the oppressed, objectified groups who are expected to stretch out and bridge the gap between the actualities of our lives and the consciousness of the oppressor' (Lorde, 1992:46).

Even when 'difference' forms part of the research process, it is easy to neglect some of the diversity within that difference. Jenny Morris (1991) cites how non-disabled feminists have failed to incorporate the reality of disabled women into research and theory. Redressing this imbalance is not straight forward. There may be a tendency to include disabled women in research but only to focus upon that which has become 'disabled' in women's lives. When this happens there is a danger that what becomes most visible is the disability in women's lives. But women with disabilities are part of our broader society and part of their lives may be their role as mothers, writers, travel agents and so on. The real challenge to research is not just to focus that which makes some of us different from others, but to recognise that the differences are all around us and probably impact on most of the research we do, if only we would look for it. If we are doing research in the area of sexuality, we should not think of participants in the research as just black or white, straight or lesbian, but also young and old, rich and poor and so on, as well as many of the stages in between. When research questions are formulated, we must the address issues of who gets specifically included within the research process and how are they represented. Implicit within these choices are decisions about those who are excluded from the research process.

Another problem which features in research is how particular groups are often asked particular types of questions. As Heidi Safiz Mirza (1991) points out, when young black women appear in research studies, they are usually asked about their struggles rather than their achievements. Thus, although young black women are made visible, it does not follow that this visibility applies to the full reality of their lives: which also includes their achievements and their successes.

Diversity in women's lives sets more implications for how we ask questions of women and how we do research. Feminists have emphasised the importance of qualitative methods within feminist praxis. But there are many issues which affect women's lives which cannot be redressed without large-scale studies and quantitative methods. For example, we still have no reliable large-scale data on women's participation in paid work. National statistics carry weight and often carry with them policy decisions about the allocation of resources. Unless feminists engage in how national statistics are put together and challenge some of the assumptions they contain, we will continue to be mis-represented. We simply do not have reliable surveys and large scale research on so many aspects of women's lives, and we cannot afford to ignore quantitative approaches to research.

Research methods

Methodology has been the focus of much discussion and debate amongst feminists. One aspect of this discussion has been to focus upon power relationships within the research process. Diversity and difference in women's lives have implications for how power might be experienced. Power is not a constant within the research process but changes with different aspects of doing of research. It is not always the case that power rests with the researcher throughout the research process since researchers do not always occupy the power position within the

31

research context. Interviews with elites are an obvious example where power positions are unclear (Hunt 1984, Klatch 1988). Even in this case, as the research situation evolves the power position may shift from the researched to the researcher or vice-versa as the doing of research transforms into the writing of research.

Gatekeepers can influence power dynamics in both directions, but there are some research situations where gatekeeping is meaningless since the nature of difference is such that only being a member of a particular group permits access to a research setting. Thus a researcher can only reflect on being young in the context of doing research with older women. Reflexivity is one way of analysing and conceptualising aspects of difference within research. This is also part of locating oneself within the research process. But there are many ways in which we can locate ourselves within research. It may be in terms of our institutional base (or lack of it), our political base, or how we choose to identify ourselves and so on. The problem with any of these 'locations' is that they are usually defined from the positions of the powerful by those who occupy less powerful positions. Thus a researcher may locate herself within the research process as black, but it is rare for someone to locate themselves within research as a white, able-bodied, euro-centric heterosexual woman *and then explore the implications of those aspects of identity.*

Analysis and dissemination

Part of feminist research is to make women visible. I have argued that visibility as a woman is not in itself enough. We should also be striving to make visible the difference and diversity of women's lives. Feminist research is also about change. Part of that change can come from within the process of doing research. But there is considerable scope for wider change. If the wider academic community continues to ignore feminist scholarship, there are limits to how much of the broader education we can undertake. From the point of view of wider change for women in society, it is not just the case of having the knowledge and expecting change to follow. Unlike natural sciences, new discoveries in the social sciences do not herald the end of the old ways. Patriarchy holds more power.

If feminist research is to provide a radical re-think of social research, I have shown that there is a need to return to the drawing-board in many aspects of what has been considered to be feminist research. The debate will continue as to whether or not the problem lies within feminism, or whether a broader re-think is required. There is evidence within the arena of women's studies that feminism will address the diversity of women's lives. Ultimately the research feminists do must be for women, and should therefore be accessible to women in different forms. Feminists should not confine their output to scholarly journals but also find new ways of dissemination which reach those who participate in research but who may never know of its findings. We can publish widely in women's magazines, community papers and so on. We can talk to local meetings, seminars, lectures, conferences, politicians and so on. There is scope to disseminate feminist research in many directions and at many levels. As women's voices are increasingly forming part of research studies, there is an urgent need for those voices to be heard. There remains much work and re-thinking to be done.

Notes

[1] An earlier version of this chapter was presented as a paper presented at the Fifth International Interdisciplinary Congress on Women, Costa Rica, February 1993.

References

Allen, S. Anthias, F. and Yuval-Davis, N (1991), 'Diversity and Commonality: Theory and Politics' *International Review of Sociology* 2:23-28

Bowles, G. and Duelli Klein, R. (1983), *Theories of Women's Studies* London: RKP

Brah, A. (1991), 'Difference, Diversity,Differentiation', *International Review of Sociology* 2:53-71

Bunch, C. (1988), 'Making Common Cause: diversity and coalitions', in Christian McEwen and Sue O' Sullivan (eds), *Out the other Side*, Virago

Denzin, N. K. (1970), *The Research Act in Sociology,* London: Butterworths

Eichler, M. (1988), *Nonsexist Research Methods,* Boston: Allen and Unwin

Fonow, M. and Cook, J (eds) (1991), *Beyond Methodology: Feminist scholarship as lived research*, Bloomington and Indianapolis: Indiana University Press

Goffman, E (1961), *Asylums,* New York: Doubleday

Graham, H. (1993), *Hardship and Health in Women's Lives* Hemel Hempstead: Harvester Wheatsheaf

Hammersley, M. (1992), 'On Feminist Methodology', *Sociology* vol 26:2 187-206

Harding, S (ed) (1987), *Femininsm and Methodology,* Bloomington and Indianapolis: Indiana University Press, Milton Keynes: Open University Press

Hooks, B (1989), *Talking Back*, London: Sheba

Hooks, B. (1982), *Ain't I A Woman: Black women and feminism*, London: Pluto Press

Hunt, J (1984), 'The development of rapport through negotiation of gender in fieldwork among police' *Human Organization* 43(4): 283-96

Klatch, R.E. (1988), 'The methodological problems of studying a politically resistant community' in R. G. Burgess (ed), *Studies in Qualitative Methodology* JAI Press, Greenwich CT and London

Kuhn, T.S. (1962), *The Structure of Scientific Revolutions,* Chicago: Chicago University Press

Lorde, A. (1992), 'Age, Race, Class and Sex: Women Redefining Difference' in Crowley, H and Himmelweit, S. (eds) *Knowing Women: Feminism and Knowledge,* Polity Press Cambridge

McCall, G. and Simmons, J. (1969), *Issues in Participant Observation* New York: Addison-Wesley

Morris, J. (1991), *Pride Against Prejudice: Transforming attitudes to disability*, London: The Women's Press

Oakley, A (1975), *The Sociology of Housework*, Oxford: Martin Robertson

Oakley, A. (1981),'Interviewing Women: A Contradiction in terms' in H Roberts *(op cit)*

Oakley, A (1984), *The Sociology of Housework*, Oxford: Basil Blackwell

Rich, A (1992), 'Toward a Woman-Centred University', in M Humm (ed) *Feminisms A Reader* Hemel Hempstead: Harvester Wheatsheaf

Roberts, H (ed),(1981), *Doing Feminist Research*, London: RKP

Safiz Mirza, H. (1991), *Young Female and Black*, London: Routledge

Shipman, M. (1988), *The Limitations of Social Research* Harlow: Longman

Sjoberg, G.(1967), *Ethics and Politics of Social Research*, London: RKP

Smith, D (1987), 'Women's Perspective as a Radical Critique of Sociology' in S Harding ed. *op cit*

Smith, D (1988), *The Every Day World as Problematic: a feminist sociology* Oxford: Open University Press

Stanley, L (ed), (1991), *Feminist Praxis: Research, theory and epistemology in femininst sociology*, London: Routledge

Stanley, L and Wise, S ,(1983), *Breaking Out: Feminist Consciousness and Feminist research*, London: RKP

Thornton Dill, B (1987), 'The Dialectics of Black Womanhood' in S. Harding (ed) *op cit*

3 Race and ethnicity in social work: Some issues for anti-discriminatory research

Ravinder Barn

This paper outlines the methodological conflicts and constraints in conducting anti-discriminatory research. It draws from the experiences of empirical research conducted in 1987 in one Local Authority Social Services Department. Issues stemming from the formulation of the research design and problems inherent in negotiating research access to bureaucratic organisations are examined within an anti-discriminatory framework.

The first question one may ask is, Are we abandoning the notion of objectivity if we espouse the principles of anti-discriminatory research? Are we allowing our prejudices, our biases, our pre-conceived notions to come in the way of 'proper academic research'? If we are to begin to answer these questions, we need to address the whole notion of objective research. Furthermore, If we accept that there is a dialectical relationship between theory and ethnography, objectivity as a concept of purity begins to hold little meaning.

The need for an anti-discriminatory research model has a historical basis. For far too long the research focus has been one-dimensional, examining the lives of the oppressed and the downtrodden. And for what? Is this the objective reality? It has been suggested that social scientists should 'stop investigating and examining people of colour', and instead should, 'investigate and examine their own corrupt society' (Carmichael 1968:174). Sivanandan (1983) suggests in the context of the growth of ethnicity studies in Britain, 'Just to learn about other people's cultures is not to learn about the racism of one's own' (p5). The power balance manifested in these studies has been particularly noticeable. Most research studies have immersed themselves in explorations of family structures and life styles, leading some commentators to assert that the black family has

37

been pathologised (Carby 1982, Lawrence 1981).

Studies into issues of race and racism in state social work cannot overlook the importance of the models of family pathology or the increasing 'internal colonialism' of black communities any more than studies into gender and sexism can overlook issues of patriarchal structures and processes. There is a need for research studies to develop an overall anti-discriminatory framework if they are to provide meaningful empirically sound information.

The Wenford study

In my study of a Local Authority Social Services Department, referred to hereafter as Wenford, the emphasis was extended to an examination and exploration of the processes involved in the admission of children into care. The practices and policies of a powerful organisation and the ways in which these impinge upon the lives of service users became the focus of attention. Issues of race and ethnicity formed the locus of the research design. With the central hypothesis being around the significance of race and ethnicity, the study concerned itself with an exploration of the contradictions and the possibilities of progressive anti-racist policies and practices.

Background to the research

The study rested, primarily, at three levels:
1. A review of the mainstream, and race and child care literature.

2. Formulation of research design to elicit information from case files, and from interviews with key individuals.

3. An examination of policy documents, and papers in the field of equal opportunities and anti-racism, and child care services and practice.

A review of the literature led to a model of research which focused not only upon the recipients of the service but also upon the policies and practices of the service providing organisation. An examination of the power dynamics between the bureaucratic organisation and the service users was considered to be vital. Moreover, it was felt that the focus upon the lives of families, both black and white, should not be from a problematic stance as had invariably been the case hitherto, but from an exploratory perspective.

There is an enormous paucity of information in the area of race and the public care system. The situation of black child care career has received scant attention (Barn 1990). Much of the literature has concerned itself with the high proportions of black children in care without adequately exploring the issues for their high presence. Since most research conducted in this area has been of a 'problem oriented' nature (that is, the high presence of black children has been perceived as a problem for the agencies), little light has been shed on the circumstances under which black children come to be represented in the care system. One of the first papers to emerge in this area was by the National Children's Home in 1954. This paper, entitled 'The problem of the coloured child', reflected an assimilationist perspective upon the growing numbers of black children in residential homes and the problems these children were creating for the homes.

In the absence of national and local statistics on the racial origin of children in care, some of the research studies have been preoccupied with documenting the disproportionate representation of black children without much explanation as to why they are there (Foren and Batta 1969; Lambert 1970; Rowe and Lambert 1973; McCulloch, Batta and Smith 1979; Batta and Mawby 1981; Boss and Homeshaw 1975; Lambeth 1981; Tower Hamlets 1982). Attempts to offer explanations for the high presence of black children in the care system have invariably been located within the black family (Fitzherbert 1967, McCulloch, Batta and Smith 1979).

Johnson (1986) has pointed to the paradoxical use of racial stereotypes by service agencies. He asserts that on the one hand such stereotypes are convenient when justifying the non-existence of appropriate service provision, however they conflict with the pathological notions of the black family - '' that migrant families are incapable of fending for themselves, make poor adoptive parents and require more intervention than 'normal families' '' (Johnson 1986:85). It is pertinent to note that whilst black family structures have been placed under the microscope, the practices of social service agencies have never been examined in a similar fashion. The number-crunching/problem-centred approach has done an enormous disservice to black communities.

Some research studies such as those by Pinder and Shaw (1974), and Adams in Lambeth social services (Lambeth 1981) have placed their focus upon the service providers, albeit in a limited way. These studies have attempted to explore the perceptions of white social workers and compare these with the perceptions of service users. The framework within which they have developed their analysis has been the orthodox class system model. This has meant that the researchers have failed to explicitly incorporate issues of race, ethnicity, culture and religion into their methodologies. The Wenford study attempted to consolidate not only issues of class and socio-economic disadvantage but specifically integrate race, ethnicity, culture and religion into the research framework. The shift in focus to examine social work practice in a powerful bureaucratic organisation became the central underlying theme to conceptualise the dynamics of the situation. Thus social work decision making became as much the concern of this study as an exploration of the circumstances of the families and children. In the light of a dearth of information in this area, black child care careers were the exploratory focus of this study.

Access to Social Services Departments

One of the major problems for this research was related to the geographical area of study. My initial intention was to explore the care career patterns of children in two contrasting local authority Social Services Departments. It was felt that by comparing the policies, practices and provisions of two authorities, it would be possible to establish the differing effects, if any, on child care career patterns.

Obtaining permission from local authorities to carry out this piece of research was fraught with difficulties. In the first year of the research, negotiations began with one West Midlands local authority where I had undergone my social work training and conducted some previous research. My previous research, while focusing on the concept of race, was of a different nature. It was designed to explore all major areas of social services provision and their relevance to black and ethnic minority communities. The individuals selected for interviews were area managers and principal officers responsible for particular areas of work. All individuals in the current negotiations with the exception of one area manager (who incidentally had forgotten who I was) had played no part in the previous study.

After the submission of the research proposal, approval was granted, in principle, by the directorate. Research was to be conducted in two of the five area offices. These were selected by the directorate. My task was to meet with area officers and social workers to discuss the research plans. The meetings with the area officers were promising, however subsequent meetings with social workers created doubt.

Social science research literature suggests the importance in clarity of objectives and the need to emphasise the advantages of the research to the agency of study in order to ensure co-operation (Schofield 1969). It is argued that the researcher should be prepared to modify their research plans to allay any likely fears on the part of the subjects of study.

In my negotiations with the West Midlands local authority, every effort was made to provide adequate information, answer queries, and allay any possible fears which may exist. Despite this however, matters did not work out and access was denied. Initially, there was no one major objection made, but a number of points were raised. These were expressed primarily in the context of the research design which was perceived by social workers to be highly ambitious. Other factors which existed were around the focus of the research which was to be in the area of social work decision-making. There was much anxiety over this as social workers felt that their work was going to be under scrutiny. They vociferously questioned the motives of higher management for agreeing to this study being conducted. In one area office meeting, social workers asserted that they would like to have a written statement from the director regarding his motives for the research. One area where workers felt that they could demonstrate power and control related to access to clients. The research methodology included interviews with parents of children in care. Social workers felt that it would not be appropriate to interview clients, or that if clients had to be interviewed, then they (*the social workers*) should have the right to veto.

Whilst I recognised the need to modify the research design to allay the fears of respondents, I had grave reservations about allowing respondents to manipulate the research to their own advantage. Some modifications were felt to be possible, and were suitably made, for example, the inclusion and/or exclusion of certain questions on the pre-coded cohort questionnaire and the social worker's right to veto access to clients at the sub-group stage. However, even after these undertakings, the social workers' position remained unchanged. In communicating the response of the social workers, the divisional director wrote in a letter to my supervisor:

I regret to say that we were quite unable to convince the staff that they should co-operate with this research project. Whilst we were able to discuss

41

with them many of their earlier fears and to allay some of them, they are still very concerned about the amount of time which they as Social Workers would have to give to this project. They appreciate that the time which they spend in being interviewed by Ravinder may be relatively little, but they are concerned that they would have to give a considerable amount of time to the preparation of children and families in cases in which Ravinder was undertaking further interviews, and in discussing the implications of those cases and the decisions made about them with her. I believe this is a very real concern in two areas which have at present a considerable number of children in care unallocated to a social worker, due to a shortage of staff....In the circumstances, I regret that I would have to support the social workers in their decision, but would in any case feel that it was less than useless for Ravinder to attempt research in areas where the staff are not actively willing to support her work.

The above decision was made after nine months of negotiations by which time work had begun in the borough of Wenford. What the above excerpt demonstrates, above all, is the nature of conflict between the front line social workers and higher management, and the fear and suspicion which existed on the part of the social workers. Prior to my request to undertake research in that department, social workers were already in conflict with higher management over issues of reorganisation within the department. Greater tension was introduced when they realised that higher management had agreed (albeit in principle) for the research to be conducted. They latched on to this as yet another stick to beat the management with. Also, a great deal of the resentment had echoes of the 'Rebecca syndrome' which Gouldner (1954) refers to as the 'Rebecca Myth'. That is just as in Gouldner's study the workers found it difficult to accept their new manager, the social workers in this particular local authority had not come to terms with their new director.

While social workers feared what they perceived to be a scrutiny of their work, there were also feelings of suspicion about the topic of the research. My previous study of this local authority's response to the needs of the ethnic minorities confirmed the inappropriateness of services highlighted in the 1978 report of the Association of Directors of Social Services/Commission for Racial Equality (ADSS/CRE). Social Workers feared that higher management had agreed for this research to be conducted in order to monitor their activities in this very sensitive area of race and ethnicity.

The negotiations with the borough of Wenford (where the research was finally conducted) began towards the end of the first year of the doctorate. As in the West Midlands authority, approval was granted, in principle, by the director, and a number of meetings at different levels took place in which I outlined the objectives of the research. Discussions were not restricted to one or two area offices as in the previous borough. In a meeting of all area officers and principal workers, one area officer stated quite categorically that due to a staff shortage in her area office, she would not have the resources to accommodate this research. The other area officers did not express any strong objections, but requested a more detailed research proposal. The presence of the assistant director and the research officer, both of whom I had met previously, was a strong influence in this meeting. They were both highly supportive of the research, and were able to express this support appropriately.

After further correspondence with the area officers, I attended area meetings in all area offices except one which withdrew at the initial stage. These meetings with the social workers were in sharp contrast to the ones in the West Midlands. Most workers recognised the need for research in this area. Their only questions were of an exploratory nature, that is, they wished to know more of the intricacies of the research design and when I was going to commence the work. Some workers made suggestions of how they would include other aspects, for example, examining cases on a long-term basis.

After only two months of negotiations, I was able to start work in one of the area offices after which I proceeded to the other two. My intention to do a census study of the whole borough persuaded me to approach the area officer who had initially withdrawn from the research. This proved to be a sound decision. One of the other area officers, having recognised the benefits of the readily available statistical information which I was collating, was able to support my case. After assurances that minimum social worker time would be taken, I was granted access to the fourth area office. Having access to the total 'in care' child population of Wenford Social Services strengthened the validity of the findings.

The cohort study took six months to complete and the sub-group interviews continued even after this period. During this time, I was also in the process of negotiating access with a second London local authority Social Services Department to do a comparative analysis. In this authority however, decentralisation was being introduced and there were various disputes over pay. Although approval had been granted in principle, the research officer involved in the research negotiations felt that staff morale was very low and that this was not

43

the right time to discuss the research project.

Due to the difficulties in the second London local authority, a third London local authority was approached. Again, approval was granted in principle, and further meetings began to take place at various levels. After successful negotiations, I began work in one area office. Here, the cohort part of the study was completed and some interviews were conducted. Negotiations were being conducted with other area offices. One hospital area office which had a very small number of children in care allowed me to conduct my work there. Another area officer appeared to be very suspicious of the research. He requested to see all questionnaires to be used in the research. Although check lists and questionnaires were made available, nothing further was heard from this area officer. There were no suggestions made to attend any area meetings. In another area meeting which I attended, social workers expressed reservations about the research, whether it was really needed, whether they had the resources to accommodate it.

Schofield (1969) stated that to avoid this situation, the researcher should maintain regular contact with the officials concerned and be the first to explain to them when things go wrong. He also states that wherever possible the preliminary results should be discussed with the officials who should be asked to comment and criticise. However, matters in the field do not always correspond with those highlighted in texts. A few weeks after the area meeting which I attended, an area officers meeting was held to which I was not invited. The outcome of this meeting was that access could not be granted due to insufficient resources on the part of the social services. There was no opportunity for me to discuss with the officials as Schofield suggests.

The situation of this local authority was very similar to the one in the West Midlands. There were plans of reorganisation within the department, social workers felt uncertain about the future, and with the departure of the director the new acting director was not much liked.

A considerable amount of time had been taken to negotiate access to the social services. Limitations on my time meant that it was not possible to approach another department. The research in the borough of Wenford had generated a wealth of information. It was felt therefore that by analyzing the Wenford data, it was possible to meet the aims and objectives of the research, and that by contrasting practice in different area offices sufficient comparative information could be derived.

Bureaucratic organisations wield a tremendous amount of power, at times operating exclusively as insular systems. When issues of race and ethnicity in the

44

context of anti-discriminatory research are added to the equation, bureaucratic power, insularity and parochialism become very clearly defined. The power of social workers and managers is exemplified in their vigorous attempts to prevent the research being conducted at all cost. Arguments such as this piece of work will be 'too demanding of our time', the research design is 'too ambitious' and the perennial reorganisations of departmental structures are put forward in the guise of valid rationalisations. These serve to create the illusion that the department is dearly committed to research and evaluation, but the present is a bad time.

What became apparent was that the powerful will try desperately to block all attempts to being researched or hinder any activity they perceive to be scrutiny. Social Services' fears about exposure to research, and what the researcher might find particularly when they themselves are under the microscope makes anti-discriminatory research extremely difficult but all the more important. Such bureaucratic organisations only feel compelled to comply with researchers when research is commissioned and funded by the government, or when they can be sure that the researcher will enhance and promote what they, the department consider to be a good record on equal opportunities and anti-discriminatory work.

Methodology

The Wenford research was based on a combination of qualitative and quantitative methods which included the following:

* Pre-coded questionnaire for a documentary analysis of case files
  and reports

* Quantitative analysis of relevant statistics

* Semi-structured in-depth interviews

* Participant observation

* Department records/documents related to child care policies, practices and
  provision.

45

It is almost inevitable that difficulties and problems will arise with respect to methodological issues (Smith 1975). For this reason, it was felt necessary to pre-test the research design.

The pilot stage allows one to test not only the pre-coded, and interview questions, but also to evaluate the feasibility of the study. For example, the number of possible categories to any pre-coded questions may need to be extended or restricted. Some questions may be rendered unusable.

The disorganised and incomplete nature of social work case files highlighted by other studies was also brought to my awareness at the pilot stage (Packman 1986, Fisher et al 1986, Challis 1987). The various gaps in knowledge suggested that it was to be an immense task to record accurate information. The ethnic origin of clients and staff proved to be quite a challenge. There were times when only after a cover to cover reading of the file that the answer to the question of ethnic origin was found. The following are examples of the indirect references to ethnic origin found in social enquiry reports, case conference notes and assessment reports:

X's mother is an attractive blonde.

As well as being physically handicapped, X is also a child of mixed-race.

There were numerous example of cases where the information had either been recorded inaccurately or had not been updated. These included the placement movements of children, as well as legal status and discharge from care. Cases of children who had been discharged from care upon reaching the age of 18 or 19, and yet according to the administrative records were still in care were common in all four area offices. Team clerks, as administrative workers, blamed social workers for not informing them of the changes. Social workers, on the other hand, did not always feel the administrative urgency of the team clerks.

The files contained very little information on fathers. This was obviously a reflection of the mother's role in the care of children as well as the fact that the vast majority of children were from mother-headed single parent families. Such omissions are also an indictment of social work investigations. Interviews with mothers revealed that there were fathers who were in touch with their children and yet social workers knew very little of their existence.

Language, frame of reference, and conceptual level of questions are important issues of consideration in the designing of the questionnaires for the interviews. It was possible to pre-test the interview questions with student social workers and colleagues who did not form part of the actual study. Appropriate modifications were made based upon the comments and criticisms by these individuals.

Research design

The research was conducted at two levels. Firstly, a census survey was carried out of all children in the care of Wenford Social Services Department. Secondly, a sub-group of 80 children was drawn from the cohort for the second level of investigation. The latter were recent admissions into care, that is, children who had come into care in the previous six months. A follow-up study of the cohort and sub-group was conducted six months after the initial inquiry to monitor progress and development.

(a) Census study

Smith (1975) points to the problem of accessibility both of samples and of the whole populations. He argues that a population is only accessible if it can be identified, and it can only be identified if it is first defined.

Definition ---->Identification----> Accessibility

Defining a population generally refers to the inclusion and/or exclusion of individuals from sampled groups. In this study, there were no samples of any type. Since it was a census study, there were no exclusions. The census study was free from sampling error, and it provided systematic control because the same subjects were studied throughout the care career process. This consistency in the subject of study meant that empirical generalisations could be made with greater freedom, accuracy and precision.

Information for this part of the study was obtained from social work case files by means of pre-coded questionnaires. The questions covered the whole process of the care career from referral to discharge. A fifteen page questionnaire containing 35 questions on the care career patterns was employed. Questions ranged from examining the socio-economic background of family to circumstances leading to admission, placement, and rehabilitation and

47

discharge. Variables such as age, gender, and ethnicity formed the central thread of the research study.

In the light of the shortcomings of previous research studies, and the methodological restrictions imposed on sampling methods, it was decided to conduct the research in such a way that the total situation could be conceptualised with greater precision. Since this seemed like an enormous task, it was felt desirable to restrict the research to a few area teams. However, for reasons of validity it was decided to examine the situation of every child in the care of Wenford Social Services Department. Also, the pilot study provided evidence that despite the disorganised nature of social work case files, the recording of information on pre-coded questionnaires although cumbersome was not such a lengthy task. The department's own figures showed that there were about 700 children in their care. The experience gained from the pilot showed that it was possible to examine thirty files in a week, and thereby 120 files in a month. This meant that the initial census study could be completed within six months. All data was collected by the author herself.

The cohort group consisted of children who were found to be in care at the time of the study in the early part of 1987. Children of both sexes, all ages, all legal routes of entry, and all ethnic groups were represented.

The cohort comprised 564 children. The pie chart below shows the proportions of children in care by ethnic origin.

Ethnic origin of children in care

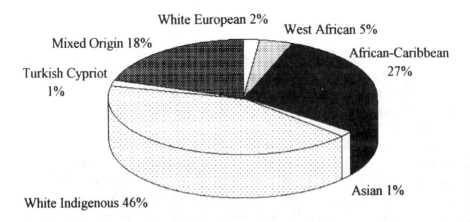

Although seven ethnic origin categories were used in the original questionnaire, the findings of the study have been racially grouped as black and white (Barn 1993). The black group consists of African-Caribbeans, Asians, West Africans, Mixed-Origin and those of Turkish Cypriot origin. The white group includes those of White Indigenous and White-European origin. It is important to note that ethnicity distinctions are made wherever necessary.

It should be stated that the two categories white and black were employed because the objective of the research was to establish whether there were differences in the treatment of black and white families and children. Also, in terms of the analysis of data, it was simpler to group the black children together in order to draw comparisons with white children. Distinctions are made within the black group to illustrate certain processes which only affect particular groups of children. The number of white European children was very insignificant and it was felt more appropriate to group them with the white indigenous children.

A conscious decision was made to examine gender aspects. In the light of previous neglect in this area, it was deemed essential to incorporate sex similarities and/or differences. Basic recording of gender on pre-coded questionnaires provided a great deal of information when this was analyzed in relation to other variables of the research such as age, legal route of entry, reason for admission, and type of placement.

The figure overleaf depicts the race and gender proportion of children in care at the time of the study in 1987. It is clear that whilst white girls have a much lower chance of being admitted into care than white boys, black girls (particularly African-Caribbean and those of Mixed-Origin) have as much if not a higher chance of being admitted into care than their black counterparts. The study found that both black boys and girls were disproportionately represented in the care system in comparison to their proportion in the general child population. Moreover, black children were admitted into care twice as quickly than white children after the initial involvement with the social services. (See Barn 1993 for a detailed account and analysis of findings of this study).

Proportion of children by sex (%)

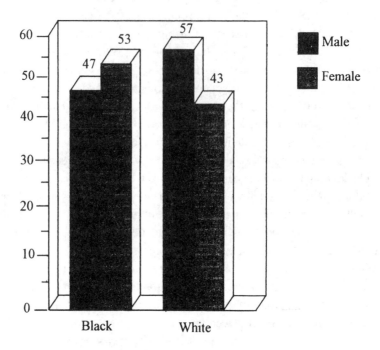

(b) Sub-group study

The cohort study produced a great deal of empirical information. However, it lacked a phenomenological perspective. This was done by means of an ethnographic account at the sub-group level. The primary focus here was to establish the perceptions of the main individuals associated with the care process. Their interpretation and understanding of the situation was sought.

The sub-group consisted of 80 children of all backgrounds who had come into care in the previous six months. There was no random selection. The only criterion applied was that the child must have been admitted into care in the previous six months. Events do not always remain fresh in the minds of individuals. The passage of time can lead to different interpretations and perceptions (Fisher et al 1986). Thus by choosing to look at recent cases, it was hoped that more accurate and reliable information could be obtained.

It was not possible to select equal numbers of children from different ethnic groups. The selection was wholly contingent upon the population being admitted into care. The situation was such that greater numbers of black children than white children were being admitted into care. Consequently more black children were selected for the sub-group. In total there were 80 children who comprised the sub-group - 55 of these were black and 25 were white. The black group consisted largely of African-Caribbean and Mixed-Origin children (28 and 20 respectively). Children from other ethnic origins were in a minority. There were four West African children, two Asian children, and one Turkish Cypriot child. The number of boys in the sub-group was only slightly higher than girls (43 boys and 37 girls).

Methodological problems and limitations

In addition to difficulties in obtaining access to subjects of study, there are other methodological problems and limitations which have to be considered. Issues of race and ethnicity, gender, age and class background of researcher need careful thought. The perennial question 'is the respondent telling the truth'? is heightened by these factors.

In interviews with respondents, personal characteristics of researchers such as race, gender, and age play an important role. Labov (1977) in his study on patterns of speech found that black children were far more verbal and forthcoming when interviewed by black interviewers, particularly ones who dressed in a casual style and who could speak the same dialect as the children. The use of non-verbal and para-verbal language (eye contact, nodding of head, and tone of voice) is also an important factor in the types of responses obtained from respondents. Many social scientists have asserted that good counselling skills such as those postulated by Rogers (1942) are important characteristics of a good interviewer (Schofield 1969, Smith 1975, Adams and Priess 1960).

Can a black researcher gain an accurate picture of white social worker perceptions? Are the respondents likely to withhold expressing their true perceptions for fear of expressing the politically incorrect in terms of race and racism? It is possible that social workers were not entirely honest in their responses to a black researcher, or felt that they had to respond in a particular way. The following unedited quote which is a response to a question on the department's equal opportunities policies illustrates this point:

White Social Worker: Yeah, yeah, yeah. I think it's an excellent idea really to keep the culture going. I think it's really important. What else. What else. I think it's really important.

Cliched responses such as the above, which became bogged down into emphasising race and culture to a general question on equal opportunities suggest the uneasiness felt by white social workers when interviewed by black researchers. However, it was clear from the in-depth interviews that such workers were not competent in concealing their true convictions and perceptions. Social workers' tendency to engage unnecessarily in a discourse on race and culture gave a reliable account of their decision making when working with families and children.

Black researchers can be particularly attuned to the ways in which racist remarks are made verbally and in writing by social workers (both consciously and unconsciously). There is enormous veneration of the white nuclear family. Dichotomy of good and bad parent is reinforced. In rationalisations such as "this Asian woman speaks no English, and would be detrimental to the children's progress", social workers appeared to be operating very much within an assimilationist framework.

Did black and white parents react differently to my interviewing them? Since parents were in a different situation, that is, they did not feel as if they had to give 'appropriate' answers, their responses were less affected by characteristics such as race, and gender. Age, however did seem important to them. Also, the fact that I was unmarried and had no children of my own led some parents to believe that I could not totally understand their situation. I do not feel however that this affected their response, they managed to convey their feelings without hesitation.

A standard format employed in the interview schedule ensured that possible bias was minimised. A checklist of points to be covered was drawn up, however respondents were not all asked the questions in the same order. The order was changed depending on the situation and the responses given to produce a more coherent structure. Such an approach meant that the focus was kept consistent. All respondents were invited to provide any additional information which they deemed important. Thus they were not restricted by the questionnaire.

While all social workers who were asked participated in the research, it is possible that the restrictions imposed upon the selection of parents and children may have biased the results. Parents' sample was inevitably biased since not all parents were asked if they wished to take part in the research. The reluctance of social workers to allow clients to be interviewed by researchers has been the experience of other researchers (Packman 1986, Fisher et al 1986). Access to clients was denied in instances where social workers felt it inadvisable for the family to be contacted, and in cases where social workers procrastinated waiting for the 'right' time to approach the family. Although there was a fairly good cross-section of parents, access to more parents would have further enriched the findings of this study.

A similar block to access was imposed in the case of interviews with children. Social workers felt that it was their job to protect the children, and that they could not allow an outsider to interview them. My own criteria, whereby only children over the age of ten were selected for an interview also meant that there were probably children whose accounts and perceptions were ignored. It is likely that this would have happened even if I had lowered the age to eight, or any other cut-off point.

Most respondents require a certain amount of information from the researcher such as the identity of the interviewer, the legitimacy of the research, the process by which they were chosen for the interview and the protection which they may expect as respondents. Also, the interviewer needs to be explicit with respect to how the information will be used, disseminated, and published (Kahn and Cannell 1957).

In the case of social workers, the information which they would have sought according to Kahn and Cannell (1957), was provided at the stage of negotiations. While all respondents were assured of confidentiality and anonymity, there were some social workers who felt that the department should be named. They argued that it would be helpful if people knew which department was being represented in the study. .

While the social workers were aware of the legitimacy of the research, and my own credentials, an official letter was sent to each parent, after permission from the key social worker. The letter very briefly introduced the research and requested an interview. It assured confidentiality and anonymity. A telephone number and address was provided for the parent to seek further information. Two mothers in fact, did feel the need to contact the university; one because she did not want to be interviewed, and the other because she wanted to know when I was coming to interview her.

In many cases, mothers knew that they stood to gain little by being interviewed. However, they felt that social services needed to be told of the experiences of parents. Some mothers were just glad to be able to tell their version of the events to an outsider. Not everybody saw me as an outsider, I was often mistaken for someone from the social services and had to re-affirm my neutrality.

Conclusion

The Wenford research study encompassed anti-discriminatory issues in all aspects of its work. Bureaucratic attempts to mould the research design were resisted by the author, which ultimately resulted in the refusal of access to two social services departments. Bureaucratic power was wielded in the guise of so-called rational arguments to prevent this research from being carried out. Had I modified my research design, toned down the focus of the research, it is quite possible that these agencies would have welcomed me with open arms; after all they were going to get the work done for nothing.

Social workers' paternalistic attitude towards their clients manifested itself in their reluctance to allow some clients to be interviewed for this study. The sensitive nature of certain cases was understandable, and interviews with these clients were not considered. However, it seemed that in other cases if workers did not have good relationships with a client, they were hell bent in making sure that the client was not given the opportunity to be interviewed for this research.

In conducting anti-discriminatory research, there are obstacles over and above the usual ones generally encountered by researchers which need to be overcome with careful work and planning. Problems of access to powerful bureaucratic organisations can influence the shape and form of research design, an area in which anti-discriminatory research needs skilful negotiations. Issues of gender, race, ethnicity, and class may be present in all research but must be consciously confronted in anti-discriminatory research. Despite the many hurdles which would inevitably come their way, the researchers must adhere to their commitment to anti-discriminatory research, and tread the path with much caution, diplomacy and tact.

Notes

Terms of reference used in the article

1. Although the author accepts the concept of race to be a social construction and not a biological entity, the term is being employed here in the absence of other suitable terminology.

2. The word 'black' is used here to refer to African-Caribbean, Asian, West African, Turkish Cypriot, and those of Mixed-Origin.

3. Mixed-Origin is used here to refer to those of a black/white liaison. A majority of the Mixed-Origin children in the Wenford research had a White Indigenous mother and an African-Caribbean father.

4. Child Care Career refers to the total process of care from admission to placement and discharge.

References

Adams, R.N. and Priess, J.J. (1960) (eds), *Human Organisation Research. Field Relations and Techniques*. Dorsey Press.

ADSS/CRE (1978) *Multi-Racial Britain: The Social Services Response*, London: CRE

Barn, R. (1990), Black Children in Local Authority Care: Admission Patterns, *New Community*, 16(2): 229-246

Barn, R. (1993) , *Black Children in the Public Care System*, Batsford, 1993.

Batta, I. and Mawby, R. (1981) 'Children in Local Authority Care: A Monitoring of Racial Differences in Bradford', *Policy and Politics*, 9(2): 137-49

Boss, P. and Homeshaw, J. (1975) 'Britain's Citizens: A Comparative Study of Social Work with Coloured Families and their White Indigenous Neighbours', *Social Work Today*, 6(12)

Brown, J.S. and Gilmartin, B.G. (1969) Sociology Today: Lacunae, Emphasis and Surfeiting, *American Sociologist* 4:283-291.

Carby, H. (1982) 'Schooling in Babylon', in CCCS, *The Empire Strikes Back, Race and Racism in 70s Britain*, London: Hutchinson.

Carmichael, S. and Hamilton, C.V. (1968) *Power: The Politics of Liberation in America*, Jonathan Cape

Challis, L. (1987) *Review and Consolidation in Brent Social Services*, Centre for the analysis of Social Policy, University of Bath.

Fisher, M; Marsh, P; Phillips, D. and Sainsbury, E. (1986) *In and Out of Care*, London: Batsford/British Agencies for Adoption and Fostering.

Fitzherbert, K. (1967) *West Indian Children in London*, London: Bell and Sons

Foren, R. and Batta, I. (1970) ' 'Colour' as a variable in the use made of a Local Authority Child Care Department', *Social Work* 27(3); 10-15.

Gouldner, A.W. (1954) *Patterns of Industrial Bureaucracy*, Glencoe, III: The Free Press.

Johnson, M.R.D. (1986) 'Citizenship, Social Work and Ethnic Minorities', S. Etherington (ed) *Social Work and Citizenship*, Birmingham: BASW

Kahn, R.L. and Cannell, C.F. (1957) *The Dynamics of Interviewing, Theory, Technique and Cases*, New York: Wiley and Sons.

Lambeth Directorate of Social Services (1981) *Children in Care*, Research Section, N. Adams.

Lambert, J. (1970) *Crime, Police and Race Relations*, Oxford University Press

Labov, W. (1977) *Language in the Inner-City, Studies in the English Vernacular*, Blackwell.

Lawrence, E. (1981) *Common sense, Racism and the Sociology of Race Relations*, Centre for Contemporary Cultural Studies, Stencilled Occasional Paper, no.66

McCulloch, J; Batta, I. and Smith, N. (1979) 'Colour as a variable in the Children's Section of a Local Authority Social Services Department', *New Community*, 7:78-84

Marsland, D. (1978) *Sociological Explorations in the Service of Youth*, Leicester: National Youth Bureau.

Mayer, J.G., and Timms, N. (1970) *The Client Speaks, Working Class Impressions of Casework*, London: Routledge and Kegan Paul.

Miles, R. (1982) *Racism and Migrant Labour*, London: Routledge.

Mills, C.W. (1959) *The Sociological Imagination*, Oxford University Press.

National Children's Home (1954) 'The Problem of the Coloured Child: The Experiences of the National Children's Home', *Child Care Quarterly*, 8(2)

Packman, J; Randall, J. and Jacques, N. (1986) *Who Needs Care - Social Work Decisions about Children*, Oxford: Basil well.

Phillips, D.L. (1971) *Knowledge From What? Theories and Methods in Social Research*, Chicago: Rand McNally.

Pinder, R. and Shaw, M. (1974) Coloured Children in Long-Term Care, *Unpublished report*, University of Leicester, School of Social Work.

Popper, K.R. (1957) *The Poverty of Historicism*, London: Routledge and Kegan Paul.

Rogers, C. (1942) *Counselling and Psychotherapy: Newer Concepts in Practice*, Boston: Houghton Miffin.

Rowe, J. and Lambert, L. (1973) *Children Who Wait*, London: Association of British Adoption Agencies.

Schofield, M. (1969) *Social Research*, Heinemann (Concepts Books No.8), London.

Sivanandan, A. (1983) ''Challenging Racism: Strategies for the 80s'', *Race and Class*, 25(2), pp1-11

Small, J. (1984) 'The Crisis of Adoption', *International Journal of Social Psychiatry*, Spring, pp.129-142.

Smith, H.W. (1975) *Strategies of Social Research*, New Jersey: Prentice-Hall.

Thoburn, J. (1980) *Captive Clients*, London: Routledge and Kegan Paul.

Tower Hamlets Directorate of Social Services (1982) *Children who come into care in Tower Hamlets*, London Borough of Tower Hamlets, A. Wilkinson

Wallace, W. (1971) 'The logic of science in sociology', in J. Bynner and K.M. Stribely, (eds) (1979) *Social Research: principles and procedures*, Milton Keynes: Open University Press.

Wiseman, J.P. (1985) 'The Research Web', in J. Bynner and K.M. Stribley, (eds) *Social Research: Principles and Procedures*, Milton Keynes: The Open University

4 Exploring ways of giving a voice to people with learning disabilities

Kathleen Pitcairn

The initial idea for this study was developed whilst working as an instructor in an adult training centre for people with learning disabilities. I believed that it was essential to create an environment within which everyone received the support they needed to develop as individuals. An important component of this was for the service users to be able to communicate with me and others around them.

I felt it was important for me to develop non-directive counselling skills, particularly active listening. (Nelson-Jones 1988). As my skills increased, theirs did too, and I began to hear and observe words and actions that did not fit with my earlier picture of the service users. I realised that when managing a group it is all too easy to organise the communication that does, or does not take place within it (Smith 1980).

When the facilitator is told that someone cannot speak, hear or remember, and all written records confirm this fact, she often never gives that person the opportunity to show that this is untrue. I began to come across instances which contradicted my assumptions, just at a time when the chance arose to formalise this observation into a project leading to a higher degree. Some time later I was able to take the investigation further, in the course of a large project which followed the progress of patients discharged from long-stay hospitals for people with learning disabilities, as they were resettled into their own local communities.

I endeavoured to be as precise and rigorous as possible in design, data collection and analysis, and in both projects success was achieved in many of these aims. However some of the most interesting points arose from the difficulties encountered. These highlighted topics crucial to understanding the history and social position of people with learning disabilities, the development of appropriate research methodology, and the knowledge of problems encountered during the resettlement process.

Context of the study.

At the time I began the first of these projects, twenty women were based in the craftroom. They varied greatly in level of ability, some could not speak, some were able to communicate easily. There were some with physical and sensory disability, but the adult training centre did not have facilities for those who were unable to walk at all. I have also worked in other settings in centres and schools with various other user groups.

The main activity at the time was craftwork, including sewing, knitting, and candlemaking, but the women also followed a timetable of educational and recreational activities, so they were rarely all with me at one time. We regularly went out shopping, to the library and to other places to encourage the users to enjoy their integration with the local community. We also helped with fruit picking when appropriate.

Speech and physiotherapists, district nurses and psychologists were available to support the centre staff, service users, their family and the residential social workers.

I was aware that the staff talked as freely with the people there as with any other people they came into contact with. The topics we discussed varied a great deal, but included the progress of the users' work, where they had been the night before, and events in the news. If it came to decisions about moves between groups, holidays, and changes in their programme, we would consult them as a matter of routine.

I was aware that some other workers, who had less constant contact with the users, were more reticent. When it came to surveys both within county and from other agencies, these were addressed to us or the parents, not the service users.

At this point I became a student of research methods. I already knew that there were many misconceptions about the communication abilities of these users. They were often seen as children who never grew up. In addition use of terms such as 'mental age', aggravated the situation. The concept might be acceptable, but the words were generally misinterpreted, by professionals as well as lay-people.

When I began to prepare my proposal I was advised that I may have difficulty justifying my choice of subjects, if I used interviewing. I was told that there would be threats to the reliability and validity of the study, because the answers would be inconsistent, and the respondents would not understand any questions. Few people had succeeded in persuading agencies that users should be recruited as respondents in major projects investigating their lifestyle, and fewer had eventually included them in their project reports, but there were exceptions. (Lowe, de Paiva and Humphreys 1986; Sigelman 1982; Atkinson 1988; Booth,Simons and Booth 1990; Wyngaarden 1981)

Another justification of the omission of service users, was that they were unable to give informed consent, as they would not understand the possible implications and consequences of being involved in a research project. (See also Bond, S 1992)

This apparent contradiction between the experience of my colleagues and myself, and the procedures accepted by research methodologists, suggested to me that this might become the focus for my own research.

At first I investigated the methodological problems, then I had the opportunity to put my ideas into practice in a major study.(Bond, S 1992) There we successfully developed data collection techniques. Crucially people without my particular experience were able to conduct the interviews with the majority of the respondents.

In both studies we discovered a great deal about the characteristics of the population, that is, those in local authority and health service care defined as having learning disabilities, as well as obtaining the information we sought for the particular projects.

There were no black users involved in either of these studies, except that I, along with colleagues began to question the absence of users from the black community in these facilities, and I believe the question is to be addressed within the local authority where the first study was carried out.

We were also able to refine the methodology further and eventually compare our findings with other studies which had developed similar approaches. (Lowe, de Paiva and Humphreys 1986; Sigelman 1982; Atkinson 1988; Booth,Simons and Booth 1990; Wyngaarden 1981)

Finally, we could see possible future developments involving the inclusion of even more users.

This chapter addresses the methodological issues arising from these studies, including the nature of 'objective' data, the usefulness of various techniques, and the notion of the development of an 'Ideal' or 'Model' Schedule.

The two studies

The first, which I will call 'The Swan Study' was carried out to fulfil the course requirements for a piece of original research for my MSc. in Social Research Methods, completed in 1988. The data was collected from residents of two hostels managed by the same Social Services Department. There were 48 subjects, 22 men and 26 women, aged between 19 and 63 years, who lived in or near two hostels, in the north of England. Eighteen lived in hostel A and 30 in hostel B. I interviewed the service users and their residential social workers.

Two of the respondents were in respite care. The remainder were in permanent care. In 6 cases there was no information given as to their length of time in care, but 10 had been in care for 20 years or more; 10 for 10-19 years; 7 for 6-9 years and 13 for between 1 and 5 years,

Thirty seven people were in hostels. 6 were in semi-independent living, and 5 were in independent living.

Degree of disability was measured in the agency records as degree of dependency. Six had been assessed as being highly dependent on staff for all aspects of their care; 19 as medium degree of dependency; 12 low degree of dependency; 6 were ready for independent living; and 4 were living independently.

The second study, which I refer to as 'The Lifestyles Project', was an evaluation of Care in the Community provided for people moving out of two large and one small, long stay hospitals in the North of England. This was a long term project, planned to last 3 years, which monitored the process of resettlement of all those selected to move into five local authorities during that time.

To avoid influencing the process of identification of movers and selection decisions, we normally recruited to the project, upon being notified that an individual had been selected. In all, detailed data was collected from 119 subjects, 84 of these were potential movers. Thirteen were included who had left hospital before the study began as they lived in the same residences as other movers.

There were eventually, four groups, those selected who moved, (movers, n.46), those selected who were delayed (n.22), those selected who were deselected, and expected to stay in hospital for the foreseeable future,(n16) and a group who had not been selected for resettlement (n22).

Virtually all who moved were able to respond to an interview. The other techniques we devised were less refined as they were not needed for direct data from our main concern, the 'movers'. They were, however, useful secondary

62

data sources and important as part of the overall ethnographic approach that we employed, whilst using more structured and positivist approaches within this.

We were able to immerse ourselves for two years in the institutions and communities during the data collection phase, which meant that we collected information in many informal ways, in addition to those using the formal instruments. Whilst still retaining our identity as independent researchers we had many chances to observe the process, and establish relationships with all involved.

Inspiration.

In the context of the Swan Study, the atmosphere in the craftroom of the adult training centre was informal, and during discussion sessions and chat over the craft activities, it became apparent that people often recounted their memories. They were by no means passive in their acceptance of the effect on them of changes in care policies and expressed their own views clearly.

For example one woman had been assessed as unable to do anything except sit and watch and walk a little. An acquaintance had said of her that she would sit and watch the blank screen of the T.V. without being aware it was not on.

This same woman began to join in the group sessions and talk a little in spite of physical difficulties. The first tangible indication of a need to question previous assessments was to see her responding to the direction of the physiotherapist by attempting the correct movements.

I decided to attempt to teach her to sew, and she learned quickly to do tapestry stitch. From then on she spent her days making a simple bookmark. She worked very slowly as the physical movements were so difficult for her, but she was able to follow a simple design and ask for a change of wool colour at the correct time, and was sometimes able to thread her needle. Her achievements seemed to give her confidence to speak more, and in turn we responded by seeking more activities for her.

Eventually she was reassessed as having a physical disability rather than learning disabilities.

It is notable that in spite of the fact that normal interactions had been denied her, she had been able to develop in such a way that when contact was made she could respond, even though she was by then 38 years old.

This sparked my interest and it began to emerge that this was by no means an isolated instance. In seeking possible theoretical bases to the investigation, I initially decided to consider this phenomenon in the light of the symbolic interactionist approach. (Charnon 1992)

Here was a woman labelled and marginalised by other people. The interaction with her had apparently been minimal and often inappropriate throughout her life, yet when I made contact with her, her identity appeared to be intact and I was able to relate to her. She had somehow resisted the negative label and developed her identity without taking part in conversation.

How extensive was this amongst this population?

The methodologist's task was to investigate to what extent it was possible to develop existing data collecting techniques to enable other people to understand the perspective of people like this woman, and include them in future research projects on equal terms with other respondents.

The two studies

Data collection

The Swan project was built upon a foundation of participant observation. The design incorporated elements derived from interpretive and positivist approaches. Data collection was conducted in ways that included both traditions. Some structured and some open ended questions were devised and an attempt was made to evaluate the various techniques.

Each interview was audiotaped in an attempt to detect any interviewer bias, as the researcher was also the interviewer.

The Lifestyles project was an evaluation of community resettlement and services for people with a learning disability, leaving long-term hospital care in one regional health authority. A comparative approach was adopted utilising a nested case-study design. (Nachmias and Nachmias 1992). Data collection was carried out over a period of two years.

Again we audiotaped the interviews, the researcher/ interviewers transcribed and dictated them, and they were entered by the secretarial staff onto a database ready to be analysed using 'Ethnograph'. Two researchers conducted the interviews. We felt that our general basic counselling training was a vital skill in preparing us to enable people who had little previous experience of being interviewed, to express themselves. It also made us aware of their reactions, and although the schedule did not probe any sensitive areas, such individual attention evoked confidences from both clients and staff. We were in a situation in which we had to handle some strong emotions from both these groups. As a result our ethical position had to be considered with care.

A videotape was made as a training exercise, which initially helped to monitor and evaluate the technique. Along with audiotaping this acted as a check on validity of responses and transcription.

Research design

A field study using interviews and observation was selected as the basis of the research design for the Swan project. This allowed a range of methods and techniques to be tested within the investigation to find those applicable to interviewing people with learning disabilities, and improve the design of research instruments as a contribution to methodology.

The initial idea was to conduct a series of structured conversations, which would be expected to be fairly lengthy and appropriate to each individual. Taking into account the difficulties in communication expected, provision was made for the inclusion of any aid to communication necessary.

There were two general objectives and within these further specific objectives.

The first general objective was to create an interview schedule which asked five simple basic questions in various ways. It was hoped that taken together, the design of the schedule and of the process of testing would make it possible to distinguish the relative merits of different techniques of questioning and also identify any aids necessary to assist the respondent to make her answer understood.

More specifically the objectives were, firstly to establish whether certain types of questions were answered or not answered by particular individuals and by identifiable groups of potential respondents; secondly to establish the value of using techniques of questioning other than conventional verbal ones, that is the use of drawing or picture cards as alternative non-verbal forms of answering; finally to establish the value of using various types of question structure. Depth, open ended and structured questions were included to see if one form of questioning proved more suitable for particular sections of the sample.

The second general objective was to monitor the adaptations to the structure and content of the schedule during the interview process in order that the need for such adaptations to the design of future schedules could be assessed.

I investigated the extent and nature of adaptations to both the enquiry and response process, as well as those within the interaction between interviewer and respondent.

Throughout both designs, features were incorporated which conserved as much data as possible to avoid the need to precode and to place a prior theoretical framework on what is essentially an investigation into a new field. I was seeking to generate hypotheses and cut across any preconceptions about the ability of people with learning disabilities to communicate in an interview situation.It was hoped that it may be possible to eventually generalise findings to other groups, rather than assuming that this is a particularly different section of the population.

As a way of investigating this possibility I replicated techniques employed in other studies. The twenty statements test to discern the respondents own personal identity was developed by M H Kuhn at the University of Iowa between 1946 and 1963. (See McNeill & Townley . (1991) for discussion of this).

I also used drawing a human figure and using card-sorts as an aid to response.

In addition within both studies I looked at the questions that the respondents asked and found that they compared closely in topics with those recorded by Ann Oakley when she talked to women.(Oakley 1981)

Such questions can also be used as another means of checking information about the respondents. Their values, interests, perception and concepts are spontaneously revealed through unsolicited questions.

These questions re-emphasised the comparison of the behaviour of this group with other samples from the general population.

The place of objective data

Both studies for different reasons began with a commitment to gather data which could be said to be 'objective,'

The Swan study required accurate information about the background characteristics of the individual subjects to assess the degree of validity of their answers.

The conditions recorded were Down's Syndrome, Epilepsy, Cerebral Palsy and combinations of these. The returns from staff questionnaires were; 19 people where none of these were recorded, 18 who displayed Down's Syndrome.

66

4 with cerebral palsy. 7 subjects were said to have had fits, 3 of these also had cerebral palsy and 1 Down's Syndrome. There were several cases where the staff responses indicated that they were unable to describe the condition clearly and sometimes a comparison with records revealed discrepencies in their responses. I concluded that this threatened the validity of their other responses.

There was also a tendency to find subjective/ highly reactive measures of development in use. I was able to compare the staff answers to a question about the users' clarity of speech with my own assessment during interviews. They were audiotaped so it was possible for my assessment to be checked. This was such a measure and would give some indication of whether staff gave an accurate judgement of the ability of a user to take part in the interview. In practice they are sometimes required to make such decisions.

During the interviews the clarity of the respondents' speech was recorded. The success of the interpretation process depends on both the actual physical prowess of the respondent and the experience of the hearer/interpreter with that individual or group of individuals; so it is possible that an untranscribable output could be transcribed in other circumstances. It should not be assumed that the respondent is uninterviewable.

Thirty six people (75%) were judged by the staff to have clear speech so I would understand them. Six people were understood by staff and residents, but it was suggested I might need to use an interpreter in these instances (12.5%). Five people (10.4%) were little understood and one had no speech, so even the staff and residents could not help in these cases.

In the end I spoke to everybody and was able to ask them all some questions and understand some responses.

It was apparent that large numbers of the responses were clearly understood, a total of 1001 utterances of a possible 1553. (64.5%)

Of those which were not clear only 19 responses(1.23%) were not transcribable by the interviewer. Two hundred and ninety seven responses (19.12%) were said to be unclear, but understood by the interviewer, so they said enough to know their answer.

One hundred and twenty four (7.98%) responses did not involve the use of speech,including some where there was no reply and some where the answer was indicated in other ways, such as gesture, writing, drawing, and sign language. It is calculated that over 90% of the answers were at least partly understood by the interviewer.

If I had used the judgement of the primary carers I would have omitted 12 people who were able to respond to at least some questions.

67

I began to think that we must recognise that this data which we had assumed to be a baseline from which we could check other data from the users, had, itself, limitations of validity. It could not be relied upon to check the status of information given by the respondents as had been intended.

In the Swan project this led to an early decision to place more emphasis on observation of the responses of the users rather than comparing the accuracy of the information they gave in their answers with that given by the primary carers. This allowed me to report in detail on how they responded to the interview process.

In the early days of the Lifestyles project an attempt was made to draw a matched control group of people who were expected to stay in the hospital. In this case the information for this exercise was to be drawn from the hospital databases. We expected a high degree of accuracy in data drawn from hospital records and staff questionnaires. As it was, even records of date of birth included examples of contradiction from one source to another, repeating my experience in the earlier study.

These included twins apparently born ten years apart. A man in one record was born in 1914 and in another in the 1920's. The latter case was discovered by a carer during interview and it had important implications for future care management for that individual.

A man who was assumed to be profoundly disabled, deaf and non-communicating, wrote his name and gestured that that was him. Another woman had recently been found to be a BSL (British Sign Language) user, although she had been assumed noncommunicating. These were just a few instances of those revealed during these studies, and supported experiences reported by other researchers.

So we have three interesting points:

Firstly, the absence of basic information given to primary carers - correct name of user, age, reason for placement, nature of disability, the user's life histories including the names of their friends.

Secondly, this can lead to confusion to the carers in the community placement, sometimes resulting in inappropriate case management because they are working within their own perceptions, expectations and interpretation of the user's behaviour, influenced by the information they have received.

Finally, this leads to the question of assumption that data gathered by professionals is likely to be accurate, and can therefore be used to check the validity of data gathered from the users or as a source of objective information on which to build a study database.

As we interviewed all the actors in the process through higher management, qualified and unqualified staff of different disciplines, some families and users, we discovered that they all varied in their ability to answer our questions. We were able to observe that as they were dependent on each other and upon their historical counterparts over up to eighty years in compiling the information about the users, there were many points at which inaccurate and subjective information could have entered the records. Added to this we were dependent upon the ability and willingness of the various respondents to sift that information available to them.

Although it is possible to trace individual case histories back to birth, it takes a great deal of time. Despite the considerable facility to see files in both studies, time restrictions meant there are still many instances of missing data, especially in cause and extent of disability, so other techniques were needed to achieve our aims.

Developing the ideal interview schedule

It was now apparent that at least some of the population of people with learning disabilities could be interviewed. The Swan project studied the ways to include as many people as possible. The Lifestyles project began from the assumption that this would be successful with those expected to leave hospital, so included a schedule in the design and also developed ways to gather further data from people with limited verbal skills.

The Swan study was about interviewing so the schedule was designed to elicit information about the nature of the respondents' answers.

It was possible that ability to answer would vary according to the type of question asked. Within the study all questions were categorised as either investigating personal facts, facts about themselves in relation to other people, opinions, feelings or memories.

Five simple questions were devised to represent these. Who are you? Where do you live? What do you like to eat? What can you remember about the past? What makes you happy and sad?

The plan was that each of these was asked in different style of interview technique. Structured and open ended questions were included, as well as those called ''depth questions'', where extra stimulus questions and encouragement were given to provide more extensive information.

Although this study uses interviewing, it is also an observation of the interviews.

69

There follows a table illustrating the matrix. In the lower section the respondent is given the opportunity to answer a version of each question verbally, by drawing, and with picture cards.

As well as key questions, there are some included for tension release or to improve the flow of the schedule.

The key questions could also act as a measure of reliability as the same questions are asked several times in different ways. .

Type of question	SELF	COMMUNITY	OPINION	MEMORY	FEELING
Structured					
Open-ended					
Depth					
Response by					
Verbal					
Card Sort					
Drawing					
Key questions	Who are you?	Where do you live?	What do you like to eat?	What can you remember about the past ?	Do you get happy & sad?

Table 1. Matrix used as the basis of the schedule design

Direct comparison with conventional interviews

The 20 statements test and 'draw a man' were included as they have been used with various populations and could possibly be used as a method of comparison with other groups. Drawing was intended as one measure of ability or

70

maturity. It gives some indication of the respondent's visual perception.
Also included are questions which required the subject to rank choices best to worst.

The questions asked by the respondents were noted and analysed, replicating the procedure developed by Ann Oakley and described in 'Interviewing Women' (Oakley 1981).

Much of this was never fully analysed, but they proved to be useful techniques and elicited data.

The aim was to collect as much information as possible, whilst keeping the time of the interview to about 30-45 minutes.

The lifestyles study

Here, as well as designing the schedule in such a way as to allow analysis using both 'Ethnograph' and SPSSx, the questions about the domains central to the study became the key questions in the matrix.

These were : Self Image, Environment, Privacy, Possessions, Routine, Control of Money,Opportunity to make Choices, Social Networks, Skills for Independent Living, Leisure.

A decision was made at first that the mode of communication would be verbal as it was expected that those being prepared for discharge could all respond verbally, so type of response was omitted from the design of the SPSSx analysis. We did soon find that this was not sufficient, but as analysis had been organised we adjusted to this by adding a new instrument. This was in the form of an outing analysed as an active interview, which will be described later.

We did monitor clarity of answer in the interview; whether we understood it (i.e. it was 'transcribable') or if the reason for missing data was no response.

A focused design was chosen assuming that this was likely to give optimum reliability and validity. It was basically structured to allow replication hence enhancing reliability, whilst allowing the respondent to answer in the way that is natural to them, so facilitating an increased degree of validity.

Observation of interviews

In the Swan Study the analysis of the responses was performed using another matrix. Each response to each question was entered, coded in six ways.
1. Amount of rephrasing necessary for subject to understand.

71

2. Form of answer given, short or detailed.

3. Type of answer, verbal, drawing or picture sort.

4. Clarity of speech

5. Did they answer the question asked.

6. Other responses, resistance,and questions.

The first observation was:'Adaptation of the Language of the Question'
It was intended that each question be asked exactly as written in the schedule and time given to answer.

If there was then no response the interviewer could use other wording or encouragement as needed. This was done sparingly with experience and sensitivity to the particular situation.

This approach acknowledged that interviewers do adapt in response to the respondent, and the extent of this was closely monitored as a crucial potential variable as the aim was to develop the 'ideal' schedule .

Over the whole schedule only 173 (11.38%) instances of adaptation of the language of questions were necessary from a total number of 1520 questionings. It is therefore possible to conclude that it was possible to interview the majority of people in the sample using a schedule with a wide range of question.

Next I looked at 'Form of answer given'. This variable was included to investigate whether when conducting an interview with this population we could expect the same responses as with other groups. We would expect a structured question to elicit a short, direct answer, from an open ended question answers should bewithin the range of choices and slightly longer. The depth questions were expected to be answered more extensively without sub-questions or prompts.

The most noticeable feature of the data is the very high proportion of short answers given. This represented a total of 1057 answers, 68.2% of all answers, when I expected this to be 53.3% of all the answers

	No of possible answers	Actual No	Expected %	Actual %
Short	836	1057	53.3	68.2
Medium	298	192	19.8	12.4
Long	420	287	27.03	18.5
None	0 expected	16	0	1.03

The high number of short answers is clear however.

72

A noticeable feature was that many of the depth questions were given a series of short statement answers; in future a code for this should be included, as this was a different response to a short direct answer.

Next 'Type of answer'.

This refers to the way in which the respondent answered; verbally, or non-verbally using drawing or picture cards in the main, although gesture, signing, symbol board, signing and writing were also noted.

Most of the respondents gave verbal answers even when picture cards or drawing were the intended medium of response. Some gave only verbal answers and disregarded the aids.

Answer type	possible total	actual total	included%
Verbal	1099 (72.69%)	1158	87.63
Drawing	188 (12.43%)	149	9.85
Pictures	205 (13.56%)	149	9.85

Of all drawing questions 79% include drawing in the answer. Picture cards were understood and used to respond in 72.68% of cases, whilst on the same measure 105.37% included a verbal answer. It could normally be predicted that many respondents would use speech, but provision was made for alternative means as this was expected to be a problem.

Only 134 answers did not make use of words.

To give some actual examples:
'Can you draw a room you would like to live in and tell me about it' is a good example -

     17 people gave only a verbal answer.

     21 did draw though some used gesture or words as well.

     6 only drew.

Except in the final question, which involved the use of a set of pictures of local landmarks where the data is recorded as predominantly verbal (36 responses out of a total of 42 being verbal, 2 were cards only), the picture cards elicited few verbal only answers.

I have discussed 'Characteristics of speech' already but to summarise here; it was apparent that large numbers of the responses were clearly understood-1001 utterances of 1553. (64.5%)

The previous staff assessment judged 75% of the subjects as having clear speech. However only a small proportion were not understood and 19 responses(1.23%) were not transcribable by the interviewer.

It was calculated that over 90% of the answers were at least partly understood by the interviewer.

The interview setting may be seen as an example of a 'professional-lay encounter' (Atkinson 1982 quoted in Silverman 1985) who point out that, unlike natural conversation, the professional sequences a chain of questions and answers with a single topic in focus.

As this type of interaction is expected, it can be used as the basis of coding the answer in relation to its correspondence to the subject of the question. We can make predictions as to the answer we would expect and that it will bear some relationship to the question.

They corresponded in 1265(81.25%) out of 1557 responses observed .

We could detect any misunderstanding of language or Yea-Saying. This is a reluctance to express negative opinions. This could be caused by inexperience of the interviewees in giving their own opinions.

Finally 'Responses of subject besides the answer'. These concern the observations to be made of the interaction between interviewer, respondent and possibly any interpreter within the interview setting. In particular they refer to the refusal or reluctance to answer the questions, and questions asked by the respondent of the interviewer.

The largest number of responses did not include any resistance 1298(84.89%) out of 1529 recorded responses.

There was one large category - resistance or refusal to answer. In future these should be recorded as two separate categories, as it was observed that some questions were resisted more than others.

The drawing questions showed the highest resistance and refusal rate. In drawing a room, refusal is recorded in 16 cases of 43 respondents asked the question. Two other drawing questions were resisted 8 times each, they involved drawing food and a self portrait. For 'Draw a man' only 6 instances of refusal or resistance are recorded of 44 responses. This may indicate that the respondents did not feel capable of performing the task in the other cases.

The different indicators of responses other than the answer fall into 3 main groupings:-

A) Over the whole study there was a total of 115(7.52%)instances of resistance to answering.

B) Four asked to go to the toilet which could also be associated with tension and resistance, but in so few instances it was more likely to be genuine need.

C) The other section of this category was the questions to the interviewer. Most of these were 75 requests for help with answer including clarification, followed by 24 requests for information about the interviewer herself. Requests for general information and for approval numbered 13 in each instance. There were 4 occasions when general advice was sought, 5 questions about the research, and on 5 occasions I was asked 'Do I need to answer?'

In some cases more than one question was asked by the respondent within the time for a question on the schedule, but only one was coded. Therefore more questions were actually asked by respondents than is at first apparent from these figures. There were also questions in the settling in period and after the session which are not accounted for here, as recording did not always begin from meeting the respondent.

These questions are an important finding for several reasons. They can be used to re-emphasise the comparison of the behaviour of this group with other samples from the general population.

Techniques

As indicated in the previous section the approach we took alerted us to the possible inaccuracies in the information we were given. In both cases the design was adapted so that it was as dependent upon our own observations as on existing databases and staff interviews.

There were some users who were literate, accurate and knowledgeable informants with excellent verbal communication skills. There were some staff who did not have the information available to them, did not understand the recording system or the information contained in them, and who found difficulty in expressing themselves. Some also did not appreciate the importance of accuracy in their responses, including telling us if they did not know.

Their grade and qualifications sometimes gave some indication of their access to information, but it was by no means infallible.

It may be possible to generalise findings to wider groups, rather than assuming that this is a particularly different or even deviant section of the population.

Likewise we may replicate techniques employed in other studies and investigate whether the difficulties we have found may be present, but not perceived in other interviewing situations.

The questions asked by interviewees compare closely in topics with those recorded by Ann Oakley (1981) in her work with women, as they did in the second study.

Questions can also be used as a means of checking information about the respondent; values, interests, perception and concepts.

Virtually all those who moved during the lifestyles project were able to respond to an interview. The other techniques were developed to a lesser degree as they were not needed for the 'movers'.

We did test the use of pictures of 5 faces (Happy - Sad) but these were eliminated at the pilot stage as we felt they affected our rapport with the respondents, who seemed to find them demeaning. We also felt that the respondents found it difficult to identify with cards 2 to 4, choosing the extremes.

It would, perhaps, have been interesting to observe any difference between the hospital round of data collection and that in the community, to see if they became more discriminating, but a decision was made upon the grounds that it interfered with our attempt to build a particular relationship of trust and respect with the interviewees.

There was scope for including other picture sort questions, but I felt that for many people in the hospital population, whilst they might recognise their own home or friends in a photograph, expecting them to generalise and comment using pictures of a hospital or a group of friendly looking people, was too refined a skill and prevented people who could otherwise understand and express themselves from displaying their ability.

The whole idea was to facilitate their inclusion so it was important not to use any techniques which disadvantaged them. If the time and resources had been available to do this well it could have been useful. As it was we found another way.

Active interviews

There was an extension of the interaction into an 'active interview'. It was developed from a technique used by Dagnan (Reported by Drewitt 1990). We asked the respondents to show us around the places they went to, and recorded this in both a structured, precoded schedule and a free description of the interaction. Some people were only able to show us around their residence, but others took us on bus journeys or walks to their town or village. In doing this we were able to get to know the person outside their normal home environment and it was a better indication of how they interacted with people outside their residence, which was crucial in a study which included observing the impact of various care policies and of the process of resettlement on the clients.

76

I began to devise an interview schedule incorporating both instruments and extending the options for answering to include showing us the answer.

A simple example of this being:

'Where do you sleep?'

One person might give a detailed verbal description.'Up the stairs turn right, the second bed. Opposite Bill and beside John.'

Another might take us to the room. A third might need to be encouraged to take us and might need leading as far as the room but could display a sense of ownership of space by going alone to the bed and lying down.

This demonstrates well the essence of this approach. It starts from the individual and allows them to show or discuss their perspective of their life. It may reveal or give some glimpse of their reality, which may differ from their carers' perception of their world. We accepted their right to reveal their views to us so that we could 'understand' them.

Here we are employing the interpretive perspective, we are being sociologists rather than social policy advisors, we are exploring and describing our findings, and the validity of the responses is measured against the reality of the respondent, not that of the nurses or project managers or county officers.

This view accepts that each group in the process sees the situation within the limits of their training, background and experience. They take part in a debate which is an institutionalised form of conflict using speech and other language-based forms of communication to negotiate the outcome. Skills in language and its transmission are essential and their level in an individual person is important in determining their power in the negotiation.

We observed each group and the interaction between them to build up a picture of the process. If this exercise was successful, each location could be observed and decisions made, to aid evaluation of care-decisions as to which should be implemented, using criteria which we felt were conducive to quality of life for individuals.

Conclusions

We decided to listen and interpret the views of a group who are normally regarded as unskilled in this. It became apparent that not only did we find out how the residents perceived the world as we aimed to, but as we were breaking the 'rules' we found out what they were. We stood beside a group defined as deviant and devalued, and assumed that they had a right to define their own reality, and we were made aware of the process by which their view is

77

marginalised.

The accepted reason for their ascribed status is their lack of skills and their disabilities, but I noted that many individuals were capable of much more than they could exhibit, like the woman mentioned earlier, the label was rarely questioned. There were people who were deaf who were more capable with language than recognised. Some people had been admitted for reasons of their era, single mothers, and other behaviour including violence. The main study group ranged in age from 21 to 74 years with an average of 45 years. Of those who left hospital the average age was 49 years and ranged from 25 to 74 years. Some of these had lived away from home for more than 40 years.

Many people were able to tell us about their lives, opinions and express their feelings, although the latter were sometimes suppressed until they knew us better and trusted us. In just the same way as their nurses did, they built up a relationship by asking us questions and biding their time before they talked more freely.

We were asked what happened to the data on several occasions by the residents.

Although I emphasise how like any other group of respondents they were, this is not to say that they had no limitations or difficulties. They had many, but the interactions with the wider community and in their residences was always affected by the primary label - person with learning disabilities, even when it had purely been applied as a result of social reasons rather than as it would be defined at present.

It must be remembered that in their lifetime the older users had been given other labels, which would affect their self image. Some had been diagnosed on admission as feeble- minded, idiot or morally deficient, and working in the wider community we occasionally found these terms and concepts in existence.

I am satisfied that the methods we employed allowed us to perceive the real differences between these users and other groups. We were aware that their primary carers encountered some care management problems, especially when a balance had to be maintained between the rights of the individual and the control of unacceptable, perhaps violent behaviour.

We did not evolve a way of devising a questionnaire which could be employed by all to elicit the views of this population, it needed more interpretation than that, but we were able to display a change in positive statements about their care and much of the data was straightforward in interpretation.

In the case of people with multiple and profound disabilities, we need to use all the skills of empathy and awareness of the individual developed by those working successfully with them, and there is a need for research techniques to be developed in this area.

Workers in this very specialised field are able to communicate and aid the development of people who have disability including physical, sensory differences. It should, therefore, be possible to engage these skills to extend our techniques.

People with learning disability challenge current cultural values where intellectual ability, physical beauty, conformity, the ability to hold a good conversation and be independent are highly rewarded.

These studies showed that the respondents could talk, discuss, ask and answer questions, when given the opportunity within their own experience, knowledge and physical limitations.

Further these data revealed that using a standardised schedule it was possible to elicit rich and varied data in exactly the same way as when a more conventional sample of the population is questioned.

They answered questions of all categories, they took part in interviews for the most part without interpreters and with confidence. They answered a long interview schedule without losing concentration or interest.

It was apparent that similar schedules could be both useful and fruitful within other investigations and this is only a start in understanding the experience of these and many other people with alternative abilities.

They perceive the world differently, not in a way that is a faulty version of those who see and hear. Researchers must design projects in a way that enables every respondent to express their views and aspirations. If we do this we will enable them to take part in creating their own home and lifestyles.

References

Atkinson D., (1988), 'Research Interviews with People with Mental Handicaps' in *Mental Handicap Research*. 1:1 pp 75-90

Bond S., (1992), *Community Resettlement from Hospital for People with a Mental Handicap,* Centre for Health Services Research Report No.53, University of Newcastle upon Tyne. Vol.4, An overview of the study.

Booth T., Simmons K., Booth W., (1988), The Kirklees Relocation Project Report . (1990), *Outward Bound. Relocation and Community Care for People with Learning Difficulties.* Open University

Charon, J M (1992), *Symbolic Interactionism*, Prentice-Hall

Drewitt R., et al. (May 1990), *'Neighbourhood Walks' a semi quantitative method for assessing the access people have in their community.*

Glaser B., Strauss A.L., (1966), *Awareness of Dying.* Chicago: Aldine

Glaser B., Strauss A.L., (1968), *The Discovery of Grounded Theory,* Wiedenfeld & Nicholson

Lowe K., De Paiva S., Humphreys S. (1986), Long Term Evaluation of Services for People with a Mental Handicap in Cardiff; *Clients Views*, Mental Handicap in Wales Applied Research Unit.

McNeill P & Townley C.(1991), *Fundamentals of Sociology 2nd Edition,* London: Hutchinson

Mead G H., (1934) *Mind, Self and Society.* University of Chicago Press

Nachmias,C F and Nachmias, D (1992) *Research Methods in the Social Sciences,* Edward Arnold

Nelson-Jones,R. (1988), *Practical Counselling and Helping Skills.* Cassel

Oakley A., (1979), *Becoming a Mother.* Oxford, Martin Robertson.

Oakley A., (1981), 'Interviewing Women: a Contradiction in Terms?' in H.Roberts, ed. *Doing Feminist Research*, Routledge.

Rock P. (1985), 'Interviewing People with Mental Handicaps for the Community Aide Programme'. *Mental Handicap* Vol. 13 No 4, Dec.1985.

Silverman D. (1985), *Qualitative Methodology and Sociology,* Farnborough: Gower

Sigelman C K (1982), 'Evaluating Alternative Techniques of Questioning Mentally Retarded Persons', in *American Journal of Mental Deficiency* 1982 Vol. 86 No 5 pp 511-518.

Ryan J., with Thomas F., (1981), *The Politics of Mental Handicap,* Penguin

Smith P B, (1980), *Group Processes and Personal Change*, Harper and Row.
Wyngaarden M, (1981), Interviewing Mentally Retarded Persons: Issues and Strategies. in Bruininks RH. Meyers CE et al eds. *Deinstitutionalisation and Community Adjustment for Mentally Retarded People*. American Assoc. on Mental Deficiency No 4. 1981 Monograph.

81

5   Lost in a 'straight' reality: Lesbians and gay men in social research

Lynn Keenaghan

This paper explores the process of conducting a piece of research that attempted to incorporate the views of lesbian and gay respondents. It is an account of what happens to a researcher who is 'forced' to go back to the first principles of social research. Although this paper does not present any new ideas about the mechanics of research it explores in detail the significance of the process of conducting social research. My original intention was to explore in detail how lesbians and gay men have been presented in research and where they have been excluded or marginalised in social research findings. Although this paper touches on these issues as part of the contextualisation the main purpose is to state simply the process of conducting some 'lesbian and gay friendly' research. Hopefully there is an academic response to this paper and as lesbians or lesbians and gay men together we can begin to define whether there can be a lesbian and gay methodology. However this paper is grounded in practice and I decided not to risk clouding some of the important issues by proposing a lesbian and gay methodology as a homogeneous concept.

The research that forms the basis of this paper was an undergraduate dissertation. During the first two years of study for a B. A. degree, I remained firmly in the closet; this was in stark contrast to earlier experience in employment where I was confidently 'out'. Staying in the closet had taken its toll on my esteem and on my generally cheery personality. The course requirements included research-based placements at an external agency. It was with some excitement that I went to meet the agency supervisor of my final year placement. X had been on TV, on 'Out'[1], the night before so I knew that he was gay. The programme was about lesbian and gay bereavement and so I also knew that his partner had died of AIDS. I felt that I possessed very intimate knowledge about

82

a stranger. During my first meeting with X I also found out that he had been politically active in the gay community for about twenty years. He had been a part of a generation only ten years older than me but who fought for some of the things that I take for granted. In response I told him that I was a lesbian, I was working class, (I would have told him I was white but given the face to face nature of the meeting I thought that stood for itself). I told him about a couple of incidents where I had experienced what I interpreted as anti-lesbian behaviour. For example I was told by a close friend not to visit her at home - because it caused tensions. The previous week one of her flat mates had heard me talking about wanting lesbian only and not women only accommodation and her jaw nearly dropped to the ground. This incident happened about the same time I asked a group of my peers whether I could have a light for my cigarette and they refused telling me 'We are all into clean living around here'. Two minutes later I looked over to where the group were sitting and they were all smoking. In short, during a short introduction X and I were communicating about details in our lives that rarely have a platform with our heterosexual counterparts and would never have a platform during a first meeting.

It was during this conversation that I realised how much I had suppressed my feelings about the incidents with my peers. This was partly because I had to face them every day for three years. I was the only lesbian that I knew of in my year and therefore support in the university was limited. These incidents have a place in this chapter as they reflect a shared experience of lesbians and gay men who are isolated. This statement will be viewed as uncompromising and subjective by many readers but accepted as truth by many lesbians and gay men. If you are a lesbian or a gay reader I would like at this point to say hello and welcome!

This interaction inspired me to assess what I wanted to achieve in my final year placement and research. During this initial interview the agency supervisor requested that I consider one of two areas for my research: the first was to explore homophobia and the second was to explore the impact of knowledge about HIV in the agency. The agency is part of a local authority. It provides training and support to the providers of statutory services. The fact that I was presented with a a choice of topics seems significant. I would suggest that if I had been perceived as being a heterosexual I may not have been given the option of exploring homophobia. I gave serious consideration to both proposals. I was inspired by the interaction with my placement supervisor which bought my 'private' life into a public domain. This inspiration enabled me to reject the possibility of exploring homophobia. I believe that I was only asked to explore homophobia because I was a lesbian and it was assumed that I would have an understanding of the anti-discriminatory issues that affect lesbians and gay men. It felt equally discriminatory to assume that I would be most interested in exploring homophobia. I decided to broaden my remit and utilise the opportunity of having the support of a gay supervisor to explore the possibilities of being a 'lesbian researcher'. From this point I attempted to formulate what this concept meant to me and how it could be translated into an academic piece of research which would be assessed on academic terms.

I was concerned from the outset that this role would not restrict me to exploring issues that affected lesbians only; I wanted to explore issues that affected lesbians and gay men as well as heterosexuals. I also wanted the opportunity to look at a broad social issue. In essence my role as a lesbian researcher would render lesbians and gay men visible but the topic of the research would not necessarily be directly about lesbians or gay men or about issues that only affect our lives . Therefore I took up the second proposal suggested by my agency supervisor - that was to explore the impact of HIV on the agency. In making this decision I was aware that homophobia might well come up as an issue in the process of conducting the research. Equally I was also aware of the possibility that exploring homophobia in a very small contained population may leave lesbians and gay men vulnerable. Although I took account of both of these variables in my decision-making process my choice was a positive one to explore how I could render lesbians and gay men visible in social research.

This decision marked the closure of the first stage of the decision-making process that was fundamental to this research. Having decided that I wanted to develop a model for being a 'lesbian researcher', in this instance, exploring the impact of HIV in an agency I now had to formulate the process. The data were eventually elicited using qualitative and quantitative techniques. The techniques outlined below will be familiar to many social researchers. However of greater significance, than the techniques themselves, is the process which lead me to using these techniques. Below I have explored in detail this process.

The search for a role model

The first stage of my study focussed on finding a 'role model'. I sought out papers from any 'out' lesbian researchers. I was unable to find articles from lesbians or gay men discussing research from the stance of being lesbian or gay. As part of this process I sought out papers from lesbian academics that I had met at a sociological study day, lecturers and academics that I had 'spotted' across the crowded rooms at lesbian discos, or at women's football or cricket matches, or watching 'alternative' theatre. None of the papers that I found written by these women gave any indication of the authors sexuality or interest in this area of study. The world of sociology failed to provide a role model. At the time, this seemed remarkable. Even the online catalogue in the library was no help since when I typed in that I wanted to trace the American Journal of Homosexuality it referred me to the 'Journal of Horticulture'.

As a student, at this point I felt I lacked a positive direction. It seemed that there are very limited forums for discussion about lesbians and research. Where the forums existed, such as a feminist sociological day school, the opportunities were not utilised fully. I was unable to ascertain whether such debates existed and I was unable to access them or whether such debate was indeed very limited.

Although the world of sociology provided few positive examples of work by lesbians or gay men in research the work of one social psychologist went some way to providing an explanation for this dearth of publications and visible presence. Celia Kitzinger identifies what I would term institutionalised discrimination, which at its worst, effectively acts as a censor of work by lesbians and gay men or on lesbians and gay men:

> many academics view research on homosexuality and lesbianism with a considerable degree of suspicion and hostility (sufficient that researchers are often warned that they are risking their academic careers by studying this topic). (Kitzinger, 1987 p3).

The concept of institutionalised discrimination has been extensively explored as a vehicle of sexism and racism (see Harding, 1987 and Sivanandan, 1991). It would seem it is now necessary to explore the impact of institutionalised discrimination against lesbians and gay men. We need to know to what extent this prevents us from reaching our true academic potential as well as to assess the more insidious emotional costs. I would suggest that it is not only institutional discrimination that renders us almost silent and almost invisible in academia and in social surveys. Kitzinger has identified an important aspect of censorship. I would suggest that self-censorship is another area that needs to be explored. By this I mean those occasions that we have not fought for the inclusion of sexuality in surveys, or failed to challenge anti-lesbian and anti-gay behaviour, or put

85

forward those research proposals that may identify new aspects of our lives.

For me, the impetus to stop censoring my own work came from an appraisal of who benefited from this behaviour. The first step was to assess how often I had done this, who had benefited and who lost out. In the processing of deciding to conduct my study I decided that every time we stay quiet we lose out. Every time a lesbian academic stays quiet in front of a largely heterosexual group they do so to the cost of the minority of lesbian and gay students who are coming to them to be 'taught'. This is not to be ignorant of risks. Lesbians and gay men do lose their jobs, or are not put forward for promotion. Maybe it is time to push out the boundaries of the decision making. Rather than deciding not to pursue a certain project ourselves maybe we should present the proposal to our mangers, or publishers, or heads of department, or research boards for them to make decisions. Even if the final decision is a negative one - the process of discussion begins to legitimise spending time on lesbian and gay issues. This process also stops us protecting management who may be anti-lesbian or anti-gay, from having to publicly make decisions (see also Barn, this volume on related issues regarding racism). Another chapter in this volume explores the issue of censorship. Carole Truman discusses how she was told by her head of department that she could put any one of four proposals forward for funding apart from the proposal exploring 'Is there a lesbian community in Manchester?'. She was told not to put this one forward as it had least chance of being funded. When her paper was given at a conference the ensuing debate and discussion did not focus on the incident outlined above. However at the end of the workshop a number of women approached her individually to say how they had particularly appreciated the personal anecdotes. It is interesting that these recognitions of Truman's experience took place in the private and not public arena of the workshop. Although this first exploratory stage provided me with little positive direction for my research design I felt that I established an important premise that I would not censor my own work. I envisaged that part of the research process would be in the placing of decisions to be made by the appropriate people.

Research on lesbians and gay men

In the course of looking for an 'out' lesbian or gay researcher I briefly perused surveys on lesbians and gay men. It would seem that articles on lesbians and gay men or 'homosexuals', a more common category, fall into two broad groups. Those articles written before 1970 which generally presented a pathological explanation of homosexuality (see critiques by Hart and Richardson, 1981; Browning, 1984; Hart, M., Roback, H., et al 1978). The themes generated by this body of research seem grounded in the premise that there is something inherently wrong with homosexuality. The researchers were concerned with finding out if homosexuals were sick (For summary of the [causes] see Silverstein, 1991). That there was something wrong with homosexuals was almost taken for granted and the researchers were thus preoccupied with finding out whether homosexuals could be diagnosed? The million dollar question was 'Can it be cured?' This body of research is found predominately in the school of psychology. It was not until December 15, 1973 that the American Psychiatric Association announced that homosexuality per se was no longer on their list of mental disorders (Silverstein, 1991). However the recent interest in the research into the 'gay gene' (see for example Observer, 18/7/1993) is one strong indicator that 'homosexuality' as something to be cured or in this case to be eradicated is still validated by some individuals and organisations today. I can only surmise that researchers taking this focus for their research did not have their academic career threatened!! Within this body of literature is one of the so called classics on homosexuality : 'Tearoom Trade'(Humphreys, 1970). Its voyeuristic neo-pornographic nature was of very little interest to me. What was of interest was how Humphreys portrays himself as most definitely not 'one of them'. The book is dedicated to his wife and children. This makes his credentials quite respectable -which is necessary given that numerous chapters describe his time spent in public toilets observing sexual acts between men. As for what seems to me overt voyeurism he gives just a passing mention. His wife Nancy must be one of the few wives in sociological history to get a public mention in a chapter 'setting the scene' about research. I do not think this is accidental. This is a pattern that seemed to recur in some articles in The *Journal of Homosexuality* . As the title of the journal suggests all the articles were about some aspect of homosexuality. Surprisingly none of the articles indicated the authors' sexuality. Although I would not suggest that the articles accurately represent the philosophy of the *Journal of Homosexuality* the trend I identified mirrors the stance taken by Humphreys in that the authors write about respondents or people they have observed as being separate from themselves. In this distancing the authors are thus assuming heterosexuality even if they are not themselves heterosexual. The second group and more recent writings on lesbians and gay men fall broadly into life style researchers. These studies often identify a positive gay identity. They support the rights of lesbian mothers to child custody and the need for gay affirmative education in schools as two examples. (Weeks, 1989; Cooper, 1989; Rights of Women Lesbian Custody Group, 1986). They also include methods of dealing with internalised homophobia. Publications such as 'What A Lesbian Looks like' by the National Lesbian and Gay Survey (NL&GS), 1992 go some way to reflecting particularly lesbian or lesbian and gay experiences. These publications include our experiences of coming out and our relationships with our families, two issues that particularly affect lesbians and gay men and thus are are undoubtedly important. The National Lesbian and Gay Survey not only provides a useful current anthology, the authors hope that:

> researchers of the future might understand what it was like to live as a homosexual in the late twentieth century. (NL&GS, 1992, p i).

These books provide a valuable contribution to our understanding of our own 'community'. I personally value reading life histories and herstories by lesbians and gay men for themselves. It would be interesting to know how many of these publications are read by heterosexuals. However if these publications are the only places that our experiences are being reflected we need to assess the gaps in the knowledge of the general population and to measure the extent that this gap in knowledge affects our lives.

I see the role of a lesbian researcher to ensure that lesbians and gay men are reflected in different areas of study, to see that our lives are reflected in more mainstream publications. Therefore I would suggest that her role is not solely to concentrate on studying the lifestyles of lesbians or gay men but to study the wider community at large. When there are general surveys about education, work or the division of labour in the home she can ensure that the views of lesbians and gay men are sought out and represented.

It is possible to find out what the most popular soaps are on TV, amongst the public at large, but we do not know which soaps lesbians and gay men watch. We are not included on census data, one of the most extensive and important data collection methods in the country. We are systematically excluded from the General Household Survey and all other Surveys conducted by the OPCS. Therefore we are unable to know how many of us live together as couples, how many of us live on our own or in alternative living arrangements. We do not know which job classifications we fall into or whether we are particularly affected by the poverty trap. We do not know what type of homes we live in. If

88

a move was made to include lesbians and gay men in large scale data collection then protection for individuals would have to be considered. I acknowledge that there are ideological issues that need to be considered in cases where access to information could be damaging to the 'lesbian and gay community'. However at this point it seems important to put the issue of both large scale data and general inclusion of the views of lesbians and gay men on the agenda. Once this happens a forum can be provided for ideological issues. It seems important not to close the door before it has ever been opened! Large scale data are used to influence policy making. We just don't figure!! Maybe it is not important to know what our favourite soaps are but surely we need to have some access to policy makers about issues that affect our lives - in terms of where we live, what work we do, who looks after us when we are in need. Not knowing what our most popular soap are on TV may not affect us in a direct way. Ending our days in a elderly persons home surrounded by heterosexuals who do not have any conception of our differing needs may become fundamental to our survival and dignity on a daily basis.

Every time that we are excluded from a general household or national survey someone has taken that decision. I for one would not like to decide which areas of research need to include lesbians and gay men. Maybe energy is better directed at looking at automatic inclusion in all social surveys. All national policy affects us all - we have a right to be reflected amongst the needs of others in a diverse society.

I belong to the group of lesbians and gay men who came out in the 'clause 28' era. The resounding philosophy and response to this oppressive legislation amongst many of the lesbian and gay community was 'we are out and we are here to stay'. For me, this has reinforced a very positive self identify in respect of my sexuality. In essence it has instigated a no-nonsense acceptance of who I am. I expect to be tolerated even if not accepted. I respect the generations that went before me that enabled me to be at this point in my life in my late 20's. This boldness enables me to take risks. These risks can channel my academic work to encourage other academics generally to take more notice of how they treat or neglect issues as they affect lesbians and gay men.

Defining lesbian research

The aim of the research was to assess how aware members of the agency were about HIV and how this impacted on work practice. Having defined that a lesbian methodology would enable me to explore broad issues I now had to

89

decide how the task would be carried out. As I had been unable to find a particular lesbian or lesbian and gay methodology I began to explore what possibilities could be developed from feminist theories. Given that there seems to be a general agreement among writers on feminist research that there is not a definitive feminist methodology (Harding, 1987) I considered that the breadth of feminist theory would present some possibilities in developing an appropriate methodological approach for my research.

Amongst feminist researchers it seems to be generally accepted that the experience of women is often hidden by quantitative data collection methods. Qualitative methods and in-depth interviews as methods of gathering data have been associated with feminist research (Edwards, 1993). This seemed a suitable starting point as traditional positivist methodology has helped to perpetuate the invisibility of lesbians and gay men in the same way that it has mistakenly assumed that women's experience, life chances and expectations are the same as those of men (see Friedan, 1973; Oakley, 1981). A perusal of almost any index in any health, or social policy research document will show that lesbians or gay men are not listed in the index or in any of the demographic characteristics unless the article specifically is about lesbians and gay men.

Feminist theory has been defined as 'political' rather than 'value free' or 'objective' and is therefore considered to be outside the bounds of 'science' (Gould, 1980). In some ways it was this criticism of feminist theory that was most useful in helping me to structure my approach. I considered that my attempt to make lesbians and gay men visible to not only be political but for the sake of 'truth' to be a necessity. As I have argued above lesbians and gay men have been systematically omitted from national social surveys. Thus our needs have not been accounted for in national policy making. Such an imbalance needs to be clearly redressed by overt practices.

Given the lack of supporting materials from other lesbian and gay researchers I took a very practical and pragmatic approach to the research design. In making this decision I was influenced by feminist methodology. I conceptualised that a lesbian or lesbian and gay methodology would include sexuality from the initial research design. I decided that the study would be conducted in two parts. The first part would consist of a qualitative survey consisting of semi- structured face to face interviews. All these interviews were conducted by myself. This was used to elicit ideas and to generate themes for the second part of the survey. If I was only concerned with eliciting the views of lesbians and gay men then a qualitative survey would have been sufficient. However, the aim of the study was to assess attitudes and knowledge of the training section as a whole and thus

90

included heterosexual respondents. Thus the methodology had to include lesbians and gay men and heterosexual respondents.

Primarily I sought to include the views of lesbians and gay men by locating myself as a lesbian at the outset of the interview. It seemed important that participants knew who I was from the beginning. I decided on an overt methodology of informing participants as much as possible. I wanted participants to be as clear as possible about who I was so that they would not be left with:

> no feel for who the researcher is, and clutch at any clue to know what s/he 'really wants' (Marshall, 1988 p200).

In doing this I was attempting to facilitate subjects being more open and responsive. This follows a particular trend in feminist research of breaking down the barriers between the researcher and the respondent which can be an impersonal interaction, and facilitating a process by which people get to know each other and 'admit other into their lives' (Oakley, 1982 p 58). I told respondents that I was a white working class young lesbian who was able bodied and whose HIV status was unknown. I gave these characteristics as I wanted to be as overt as possible about who I was. I also wanted to be clear about myself in terms of key variables in the research. For this reason it was important to make a statement about my HIV status as it is known to me. This also sent a message to respondents that I was aware of issues around HIV status. At the outset of the research I was keen to explore whether there was a difference in awareness of issues around HIV between people who identified as having a disability and those people who did not. I believed this reflexive account provided respondents with enough information to allow them to identify any commonalities with me but it equally enabled respondents to identify important differences. I believe that identifiable commonalities between the researcher and the respondent are positive. This has been shown to be useful when exploring the experience and contributions of black and white women, of black women generally, and in interviews of people with a disability (Dominelli, 1988). It has been particularly noted in the interaction between a female interviewer and a female respondent that female respondents are more open. This has been rationalised in that women 'share a subordinate structural position by virtue of their gender' (Finch, 1984 p76). Reflexive accounts often include class, race and sex. It has also been shown that to openly acknowledge difference facilitates more open communication between the researcher and the respondent (Edwards, 1993).

91

The approach I took is significant in that I shared personal information about myself before the interview and that I included my sexuality.

I felt that this classification of myself would enable people who did not identify themselves as heterosexual to feel that they could share this information with me. What was less clear at this point of the research design was the effect that my self classification would have on respondents who identified as heterosexual. As this was unknown I decided to monitor whether respondents perceived that the fact I had told them I was a lesbian had made a difference to their response.

The process of the research

Initially twelve people were interviewed using a stratified random sample of half of the agency. In this sample one man identified himself as gay, two men identified themselves as bisexual and one women identified herself as a lesbian. One woman and one man identified themselves as heterosexual and the remaining respondents did not identify their sexuality. Finding a lesbian and gay man in my sample was not a surprise as these two people were generally 'out' at work.

Attempting to classify respondents' sexuality was problematic because not all respondents had classified their own sexuality. Initially I developed two categories that identified sexuality: 'lesbian, gay and bisexual respondents' and 'heterosexual respondents'. Although from the outset these two categories did not 'feel right', it was only after much discussion with X that we realised that we had fallen into that age old familiar assumption that heterosexuality is assumed unless it is otherwise stated. In developing categories I was restricted by the number that would enable the data to be presented in a meaningful manner as the sample size was so small. The categories that I finally used were 'respondents who identified them self as lesbian, gay or bisexual' and 'respondents who did not identify them self as lesbian gay or bisexual'. Although a little cumbersome and lengthy this was the only categorisation that felt both useful and truthful given the information that I had been given.

All the respondents who identified themselves as lesbian, gay or bisexual perceived that my disclosure identifying myself as a lesbian made a difference to how they responded in the interviews. The two bisexual men indicated that they would not normally be open about their bisexuality. The lesbian and gay man indicated that they may have revealed their sexuality any way as they are generally 'very out' however they revealed that my disclosure had still had an impact on their response during the interview. The lesbian felt under pressure because she was conscious of a desire to be more helpful than she may otherwise have been. She was aware of wanting to put more energy into the interview because she felt that the 'truth would be told'! The gay man was also visibly nervous during the interview. At one point he asked me to stop the interview because he needed to discuss the pressure he felt he was under to give 'right answers'. This pressure stemmed primarily from the fact that he was the HIV trainer and wanted to give the 'right answers' but he also wanted to be helpful because he was fully committed to my research. The first bisexual respondent indicated that he felt he wanted to fully engage in the interview process because he thought that I would be sympathetic to the needs of people affected by HIV. The second bisexual respondent thought I was giving him a clue to my political bias - and would be approaching the subject matter from the viewpoint that 'the personal is political'.

Of the respondents who did not identify themselves as lesbian, gay or bisexual, only one indicated that my revelation had made a difference to the interview process. He said that he was able to feel more at ease about the interview because he felt that he did not have to worry about 'hidden agendas'. I would suggest that some of the other respondents responses in the interview were also affected in some way by my introduction. One respondent who showed a very low level of awareness about anti-discriminatory practice kept including lesbians in response to some of my questions in quite inappropriate places!! In response to a question asking which groups of people have been discriminated against because of HIV and AIDS most respondents indicated that they thought lesbians had been discriminated against. Some of these respondents were unable to articulate an analysis of how or why lesbians were discriminated against as a group in relation to HIV. I therefore felt that lesbians would not have been included in response to this question if I had not disclosed that I was a lesbian. The responses to this question would indicate that my self disclosure had some impact on the responses. However the responses did not affect the outcomes of the aim and objectives of the research. One of the objectives had been to explore an understanding of discrimination. By the use of strategically structured probes I had been able to assess respondents understanding of discrimination.

I would suggest that apart from the question on discrimination my self disclosure did not affect the responses to other questions. During the second stage of the interview all respondents answered a knowledge and an attitude questionnaire. Both the initial semi-structured interview conducted with the sample and the subsequent attitude and knowledge questionnaires were quite challenging. The most frequent response from respondents at the end of each interview was something like 'Oh I didn't expect to have to think so hard!'. Each question had been discussed with the HIV trainer and we had ensured that they reflected back to the aims and objectives of the research.

Members of the agency were familiar with research as a concept. The relative familiarity of the respondents in participating in a research process facilitated my research. Although some aspects of my research design will have been different to their previous experience respondents appeared to engage in 'shared status and assumptions'about research. Shared status and agreed assumptions have been identified as facilitating a quick and open exchange during interviews between middle class women interviewers and respondents (Brannen, 1988). Many of the respondents I interviewed have previously had to conduct their own research projects and most had recently participated in an earlier study. The interviews were held during work time and thus participation was legitimated by management. Nobody refused to be interviewed although in practice it proved impossible to interview several respondents.

As an interviewer, my sexuality was only part of a very carefully packaged product. Some respondents commented that they generally perceived me as being 'open and friendly' and this put them at their ease. At the time I was aware of this as a dynamic and so I was conscious of continuing to communicate in a 'friendly manner'. That the most immediate response at the end of the interview was about the challenging nature of the questions was, I believe, an accolade to the methodology. However my disclosure as a lesbian had an important impact on the findings. After much reflection on my work I think that if I had been a heterosexual researcher the HIV content of the findings may have been similar but some aspects of the research would have remained unexplored and thus invisible in the findings.

The findings of the research were not remarkable; my research found that lesbians, gay men and bisexual men were more authoritative and knowledgeable about HIV than those respondents who did not identify themselves as lesbian, gay or bisexual. What did seem remarkable was the strength of the findings. When the results were finally written up I was surprised at my own sense of achievement. This was only partly stimulated by writing an extensive research paper on HIV and AIDS but was more directly related to the fact that my findings presented lesbians, gay men, and bisexuals truthfully and in a very positive way. My supervisor rang and his pride and joy was also evident in the fact that the findings had shown his lesbian and gay colleagues in such a positive light. On rereading my paper several months later I found that I wanted to celebrate the outcome and the process that enabled this outcome. This compounded the realisation of the dearth of other positive accolades for lesbians and gay men.

I succeeded in one of the aims of the research design which was to make visible the views of lesbians and gay men. As a side product of my efforts I was also able to highlight the knowledge and views of bisexual men in the research. They had also felt safe in declaring their sexuality to me because I had given them an opening.

As I have indicated above, both the lesbian and gay respondent identified that they put more energy into the interviews because they felt that their views would be heard and not distorted. It seems significant this was the first comment that they made in the debrief session. Conversely none of the respondents who did not identify as lesbian, gay or bisexual commented on their perceptions of the outcome. This may be that they did not have the same trust and therefore did not confide in me; alternatively I would suggest that heterosexual respondents, particularly white male professionals, are possibly more used to having their views represented and take this for granted!

Some problems and lessons

As in many research projects there were restrictions imposed on the research design. Halfway through the data collection period I was informed by the agency manager that I would be unable to ask respondents about their sexuality. This rule was supposedly aimed at protecting lesbians, gay men or bisexuals from being faced with a difficult decision about whether to come out or not - by a tick on an anonymous form or during a face to face interview. I was only able to overcome this restriction because I was from an outside organisation. It seems that rather than protecting us this type of ruling may render us invisible and deprives us of choice. For some of us the ability to be open is fundamental to our existence. The bureaucratic process of challenging this rule was frustrating and took up valuable data collection time. This incident is illustrated not to deter researchers from incorporating sexuality into the research design but to show that not only is the process of the research as important as the outcome but that the process dictates the outcomes. If I had not challenged this bureaucracy then I would not have been able to explore one of the most interesting trends in my research. I would still have had a very interesting research paper on the impact of HIV and AIDS on the agency but the contribution of lesbians and gay men would once again have remained invisible.

It would not have been possible to conduct this research if important gatekeepers had not been supportive of the methodology. Of paramount importance and inspiration was the support of my placement supervisor. From the outset I considered that academic acceptance of the methodology would be the biggest hurdle. Although I had known that the academic supervisor was a lesbian, as she was not 'out' professionally it was difficult to assess how supportive she would be. In terms of gaining academic acceptance I sought support in developing a research methodology that challenged a positivist approach. Thus the research and the methods were given approval by the agency and was accepted as an academic piece of work by the University. It was not dismissed as unacademic or unscientific as other work that has fallen outside the narrow positivist criteria (Simpson, 1978).

Apart from some bureaucratic difficulties, of which I have outlined one example above, it was relatively easy to conduct the research because of the support of the gatekeepers. It came as a surprise when there was resistance to the distribution of the report within the agency. The initial resistance to distribute the report came from senior management level. A number of reasons were given: the first concern was that the report had not paid sufficient attention to confidentiality. I duly made some alterations. This criticism was then refined. The concern presented was that individuals would be able to identify their own quotations in the report. I had quoted extensively from respondents' own words. I did not perceive this as a problem - rather as a reflection of the accuracy of the quotations. I did not consider that people being able to identify 'their own quotations' was breaking confidentiality. The manager made the suggestion that I should disseminate a two page summary of my one hundred page report!! If this was done then the most important aspect - that of the strength of the findings of the research would be lost. On the third consultation about the research (all of this in my unpaid time of course!!) the manager suggested that the agency staff 'were not ready for another piece of research that reflected them in a negative way'. This then came to be the crux of the problem. I have been concerned that the report may have been distributed with little resistance if those respondents who did not identify as being lesbians, gay and bisexual had been shown to have more knowledge and less discriminatory attitudes than their lesbian, gay and bisexual counterparts. The report has stayed in a drawer for months. Without the power to disseminate, the research and research findings are of limited use. Is this an example of ignoring research as attention confers a measure of legitimacy or an example of suppressing a 'deviant influence' preferably without appearing to do so (S Wilkinson, 1988). It has only taken one gatekeeper in a position of power to suppress what my agency supervisor and I consider to be an important piece of research.

I would like to reiterate that I believe that the process of the research is as important as the outcome. I remain confident that some or all of the report will eventually be distributed. I have confidence because of the complete support by my agency supervisor. Equally if the report is not distributed then we will insist that the reasons are made public and a summary will be then be distributed. In this way the people withholding the information and thus the power will be made visible and we will not be censoring ourselves.

I hope that I have shown that in devising my methods I have clearly illustrated that I was able to include the views of lesbians, gay men, bisexuals and heterosexuals. This was done by being open about who I was accompanied by qualitative and quantitative data collection methods. I was able to triangulate my data and thus my methods will withstand the test of the traditional concepts of reliability and validity. However rather like Edwards I was not so concerned about these concepts rather I was seeking out an accurate representation of the views of all the people in the training section. Edwards argues that researchers should not be so concerned with making sure that what goes into every interview is the same to ensure reliability and validity, rather they:

> should work to ensure what comes out is the same in quality, that is, not in terms of content but in terms of gaining a validly re/constructed re/presentation of 'what is' for each subjects situation and her understanding of it. (Edwards 1993 p91)

If nothing else I hope this chapter inspires other students and researchers to push out the boundaries of social research, to move away from the restricted versions of truth perpetuated by positivism into a more creative and more accurate reflection of the diverse society that we live in. I am aware that I touch on a number of issues and have taken a simplistic approach to developing a 'lesbian and gay friendly'methodology. However I feel sufficiently confident that lesbians and gay men have been excluded from social research to warrant such a paper. I hope not only to incorporate these concepts within the research that I will conduct but to be able to read more social studies that include representations from lesbians and gay men. Hopefully as we become more visible in academia the less vulnerable we will be to the anti-lesbian and anti-gay incidents outlined above. It is only when we have made sufficient representations for ourselves that our straight colleagues will have to begin to include us seriously. Until we take the risks we will remain hidden within the 'straight reality'.

Notes

1 Channel 4's lesbian and Gay Magazine programme

References

Brannen, J. (1988) 'The Study of Sensitive Subjects'. *Sociological Review* 36:552-563

Browning, C.(1984) 'Changing Theories of Lesbianism: challenging the sterotypes', in T. Darty and S. Potter (eds) *Women-Identified Women*. Palo Alto, CA Mayfield publications

Cooper, D. (1989) 'Positive Images in Haringey: a stuggle for identity', in Jones, C. & Mahoney, P. (eds) *Learning Our Lines : sexuality and social control in education*, London, Women's Press

Cooper, D. (1989) *Fostering and Adoption by Lesbians and Gay Men*. London, Strategic Policy Unit

Dominelli, L.(1988) *Anti-Racist Social Work: A Challenge for White Practitioners and Researchers*, Basingstoke, Macmillan

Edwards, R. (1993) 'An Education in Interviewing: placing the researcher and the research', in Renzetti, R. & Raymond, L (eds) *Researching Sensitive topics*. London, Sage

Finch, J. (1984) 'Its great to have someone to talk to: the ethics and politics of interviewing women'. In Bell, C. & Roberts, H. (eds) *Social Researching*, London: Routledge, Kegan & Paul.

Friedan, B. (1973) *The Feminine Mystique*, W N Norton: New York

Gould, M. (1980) 'The New Sociology Signs', *Journal of Women in Culture and Society* vol. 5, no. 3 pp 7 - 15

Graham, H. (1984) 'Surveying through Stories, in Bell, C. & Roberts, H. (eds) *Social Researching*, London: Routledge & Kegan Paul.

Harding, S. (ed) *Feminism and Methodology*, Open University Press Milton Keynes

Hart M., Roback, H., Tittler, B., Weitz, L., Walston, B., & Mckee, E. (1978). 'Psychological adjustment of nonpatient homosexuals: Critical review of the research literature'. *Journal of Cinical Psychiatry*, 39, pp604-608

Hart, J. and Richardson, D (eds) *The Theory and Practice of Homosexuality*. London: Routledge & Kegan Paul

Humphreys, L. (1970) *Tearoom Trade*. London,Gerald Duckworth & Co. Ltd

Kitzinger, C (1987) *The Social Construction of Lesbianism*. Sage London

Marshall, J. (1988) 'Exploring the Experiences of Women Mangers: Towards Rigour in Qualitative Methods' >>>>>>> in Experiences of Women Managers

Morin, S. (1977) 'Heterosexual Bias in Psychological research on lesbianismand male homosexuality', *American Psychologist* 19: 629 - 37

National Lesbian and Gay Survey (1992) *What a Lesbian Looks Like: Writings by Lesbians on Their Lives and Lifestyles.* Routledge London

Oakley, A. (1981) 'Interviewing women: a contradiction in terms' in Roberts, H (ed), *Doing feminist Research* Routledge & Kegan Paul

Rights of Women, Lesbian Custody Group (1986) Lesbian Mothers Legal Handbook Womens Press

Silverstein, C. (1991) 'Psychological and medical treatments of homosexuality', in Gonsiorek, J. & Weinrich, D. (eds) *Homosexuality: research implications for public policy.* Sage

Sivanandan, A. A. (1990) *Communities of Resistance, Writings on black struggles for Socialism,* London, Verso

Weeks, J. (1989) *Sex, Politics and Society,* London, Longman

Wilkinson, S (1988) 'The Role of Reflexivity in Feminist Psychology' *Women's Studies Int. Forum.* Vol 11. No. 5. pp493 -502 USA

6 Critical life histories: Key anti-oppressive research methods and processes

Derek Clifford

The aim of this paper is to propose an approach to social research which draws on a multidisciplinary methodology, which is anti-oppressive, and which is particularly valuable for people who are working and researching in the social, health and welfare professions. By 'anti-oppressive' I mean to imply an understanding of social life which regards social divisions as basic phenomena which condition our lives and thought, including not only class, gender and 'race', but also sexuality, disability and age. It is therefore important to explore alternative ways of conducting research which are not constrained by the dominant conventions. I have drawn on black feminist perspectives as a guide to anti-oppressive values and have attempted to describe and justify 'Critical Life Histories' as a research methodology which meets these criteria, and which is particularly relevant for the stated purposes.

I will argue that there is great relevance in the connections between life-course and life history methods in sociology, life-span developmental psychology, and oral history, relating all three to some of the central concerns of black feminism. There have been recent developments in all of these areas, and one - oral history - has only become an academically accepted and thriving discipline in the last two decades, with one key book providing both a summary of the emergence of the discipline and a platform from which subsequent work has developed, (Thompson, 1984). It is surprising that the study of the life-course, and the life history approach in sociology has not been utilised much more, as these two closely related areas of sociology have been studied for a long time. However, it is true that the life history approach largely disappeared after its initial popularity in the 1930's, and there has only begun a slow revival of interest in it in recent years, (Plummer, 1983). Life course sociology has recently become the preferred phrase for the study of what was previously examined under the heading of 'life-cyle' and 'family life-cycle', and represents a theoretical move forward in the attempt to link biography and history, (Morgan, 1985).

Life-span developmental psychology has been growing in influence considerably over the last two decades. The application of psycho-dynamic theories to the whole life span is particularly associated with Erikson, (Erikson, 1958, 1975 and 1977), whose influential works not only founded the discipline of life-span developmental psychology, but also signalled the start of the modern period of the cognate field of psycho-history, (Runyan, 1988, pp.12-14). The use of psychodynamic theories has *not* always been made with a life-span perspective, but it is significant that the doyens of attachment theory have only recently published an up-dating of their approach from this angle, (Parkes, 1991). One of the questions raised here will be the adequacy of any psychological approach to social research which is not explicitly and theoretically integrated with appropriate sociological and historical factors of interpretation, unconnected with anti-oppressive values.

It is being consistent with this methodology that makes it important to say something about my own specific 'position'. Like many working class white males educated in grammar schools and Universities, I have gained from a period of re-education from feminist and black perspectives. This has been in the context of an extended period of involvement in child care social work, working with many black and white women and men as colleagues and service users in multi-ethnic areas. I began to explore 'critical life histories' as a way of applying anti-oppressive values to practice and research, and continue to do so as a lecturer in a social work department that has seen a small revolution in personnel since I have been there, with white males being replaced with black and white female staff, especially in social work practice teaching. To them I owe considerable thanks for their interest and advice. I am, of course, aware that I have to be responsible myself for my understanding and use of 'black feminist' perspectives. I would like to emphasise the obvious: that I do not assume that it could possibly be definitive.

I have learnt from the values and methodological criteria suggested by black feminist theorists, (see, amongst others, Bryan, 1985; Collins, 1990; Davis, 1982, 1989; Hooks, 1982. 1984, 1989; Jordan 1989; Lorde, 1982, 1984, 1988; Mama, 1989; Parmar, 1990). I am *not* assuming that there is one 'black

103

feminism': I have been interested in the way different writers have been able to analyse their own experience of multiple forms of oppression - particularly class, gender, 'race', and sexuality, and have from their own personal and collective experience been able to develop methodologies which seek to systematically take account of the variety, historical change, complexity and interconnection of social divisions. I am not assuming that only black women have insight into multiple forms of oppression, but the numerous writings that they have produced in recent years have made a significant contribution.

The common themes which I have found useful as guidelines are based on those proposed by Williams (Williams, 1989, p.80), and Collins, (Collins, 1990). An anti-oppressive method seems to need to be:

1. Anti-reductionist, and historically specific. (not reducing explanations to biology, psychology, or economics, and placing the explanation within a specific historical context).

2. Materialist, (in the sense of relating to material power structures, and the divisions of material wealth and power in society).

3. Combining personal, (the family, reproduction, sexuality) and political (work, and the 'outside' world).

4. Thoroughly analysing 'difference', (that is systematically placing individual people and groups within all the social divisions).

5. Internationalist, (understanding the wider contexts which affect us all indirectly and some of us directly).

6. Reflexive: the author or observer is accountable for the methods used and the knowledge claimed - they do not exist at some neutral value-free point outside the framework, but are part of the social action and as such, 'values lie at the heart of the validation process such that enquiry always has an ethical aim', (Collins, 1990, p. 219). The personal biography of the author is thus as important as that of the interviewee, and the dialogue which must occur for knowledge to increase is not an interference to social understanding, but an essential part of it. It is a specific role of black feminists' values to anchor the dialogue in reality: 'Personal narratives of non-dominant social groups.. are often particularly effective sources of counterhegemonic insight because they expose the viewpoint embedded in dominant ideology', (Personal Narratives Group, 1989, p.7).

Collins as a black feminist attempting to analyse black feminist thought, compares her 'holistic' methodology with C. Wright Mills' 'sociological imagination', and describing both as: 'a way of knowing that enables individuals to grasp the relations between history and biography within society' (Collins, ibid, p.230). This stress on the dialogical sharing of narrative accounts of significant events in personal histories, connecting individuals and communities within the context of social history provides a broad and satisfying theoretical framework for various kinds of social research, but especially for a 'critical life history' approach to research. Its full meaning can be elaborated further by an evaluation of the three disciplinary areas already identified, where recent developments have to varying degrees brought them into closer relationship with anti-oppressive values.

History and oral history

It is only within the last two decades that oral history has established itself with a relatively firm footing as a recognised branch of history, basing itself around new journals devoted to this method, (see Thompson, 1984). The movement has its origins in a concern with the lives of ordinary people who have not in the past featured in established historical texts. There was therefore from the beginning a commitment and interest in the lives and the knowledge of working people who did not belong to the dominating social groups, and their perspectives and experiences. The method has been able to draw on historical roots such as African traditions of oral transmission of historical knowledge.

The ability of oral history techniques to illuminate the lives of people who belong to the dominated groups within our society has much to offer an anti-oppressive approach to social research. The connections have become particularly striking with the publication of recent collections of papers which presents oral history as a specifically feminist practice, (Personal Narratives Group, 1989; Gluck and Patai, 1991). They explicitly prioritise the task of setting lives into a specific historical context which is interrogated for its particular combination of social divisions, and also examine the processes of oral history interviewing in ways that are directly relevant to the process of anti-oppressive social research. They are consistent in their appreciation of the role of oral history in contributing both to the dialogical understanding and self-awareness of people from dominated social divisions, as well as to the structural issues of social power and the specificity of time and place.

Some of the issues presented by oral historians from this perspective are as follows. Firstly, in *some* circumstances there is the liberating nature of the method itself, and its 'inherent' compatibility with anti-oppressive values:

'the telling of the story can be empowering, validating the importance of the speaker's life experience', (Gluck and Patai, 1991, p.2). A black woman specialist in linguistics claims that: 'It is oral narrative that is ideally suited to revealing the "multi-layered texture of black women's lives"', (Etter-Lewis, 1991, p.43). It has also been argued that: 'Within the human sciences, oral history - both the method and the discipline - has often been cited as *the* exemplar of how social research can be empowering', (Bhavnani, 1990, p.145). However, as the latter author warns, there is no automatic guarantee of any research method being empowering, - any method can be used to mask power inequalities, and this leads into the second area of interest for anti-oppressive social assessment. This is that feminist oral historians are critically aware of the power issues that arise in the process, content and context of their work.

There is an explicit commitment to the investigation of power inequalities in the *content* of the work: 'as an explanatory framework for a life experience, gender, ..(is) inextricably bound to class and ethnicity', (Olsen and Shopes, 1991, p.193). There is also an explicit commitment to an examination of the power inequalities in the *process* of the research, which 'places research subjects at grave risk of manipulation and betrayal', and in the 'dissonance' between the collaborative fieldwork interview and the research product, over which the interviewee has little or no control', (Stacey, 1991, pp 113-4). There is also a keen awareness of the *context* of research, its material inequalities and the social and political environment which determines that context, together with a determination that 'By doing work where we have personal commitments, our academic contributions are more likely to come out of a personal, creative, politically engaged self, one that has a social - and not just an academic - purpose', (Olsen, and Shopes, 1991, p.201).

The latter point is connected with a third issue raised explicitly by the practice of feminist oral history - the focus on reflexivity and values. A number of authors emphasise the point that what is happening is not the telling of one story, but two stories. The life history of the interviewee as told from their perspective is one story, whilst its reception and re-interpretation by the interviewer is another, (Borland, 1991; Mblinyi, 1989). This reflexive aspect of oral history is mirrored in Stanley's comments on how powerfully biography and autobiography are intermingled in the process of studying someone else's life: 'this person with this particular personal and intellectual history in this time and place who understands in now this light, and now that, first one then more facets of this other person', (Stanley, 1988, p.22). In other words the principles of historical and social specificity apply both to the researcher and the subject, and to the relationship that develops over time between them. This inevitably makes the oral history ethical and political in its implications.

Thus, oral history is a method of understanding which successfully places people's lives in specific changing historical contexts of social divisions - making the connections between biography and social structure in ways that make sense to both subjects and researchers. The perspective of one black feminist is precisely that it is because oral narrative 'reflects a multiplicity of experiences and worldviews' that it is the best suited method for understanding the experiences of black women, because of 'their multiple social roles, which are acted out simultaneously', (Etter-Lewis, 1991, p.56). A similar point is also forcefully made by women researching into the lives of other working class women: 'as a person narrates a life story, and the account wends its way through the accumulated details of a life, social categories are exploded: the subject becomes an actor in simultaneous, multiple roles that do not conform to easy generalisations', (Olsen and Shopes, 1991, p.193). As a discipline, oral history makes a vital contribution to understanding the complex detail, and interconnecting layers of meaning and influence in people's lives, and is therefore an essential component of a 'critical life history' approach to social research. The emphasis of history is upon the exploration of human pasts, interpreting human documents and human testimony in the context of these multiple details, and of the wider historical patterns and influences which bear upon particular lives.

Sociology, life histories and the life course.

The sociological tradition of the 'life history', or the 'life documents', method of research has obvious relevance to social, health and welfare fields. It is traditionally a qualitative methodology, based on humanistic concerns with individual lives and the importance of subjective perception, and was closely connected to the interpretive and symbolic interactionist sociology of the Chicago school in the 1930's, when it was at its heyday. However, there has been a continual production of life stories up to and including the present (see Plummer, 1983, p. 35) The method also has close links with participant observation and other ethnographic approaches which were also popular at the same period. Within recent times, feminist approaches to research in sociology have strongly argued that since the personal and political are closely connected, then the detailed qualitative investigation of the personal is equally important as research into wider and more public aspects of social life, *and* is crucially inter-related with these wider aspects, (see Stanley, 1990).

The essence of the life history method is that it should be: ' a horizontal and vertical reading of the biography and the social system; back and forth from biography to social system, and from social system to biography', (Bertaux, 1981, p.21). It is this complex effort to relate the individual to social systems within a temporal framework which is of great relevance to social and welfare research, and which can be easily related to black feminists' perspectives, as it is essentially anti-reductionist, specifically historical and reflexive, and *potentially* relates to the material differences between the social divisions. The method can be used in an individualistic and humanist way, but the approach being suggested here is explicitly linked to the ways in which individual lives are connected to the social structure, and especially the social divisions. Bertaux distinguishes between a life story method based on interviewing a subject about their perceptions of their own history, as against a life history method, which relies principally upon documents, (Bertaux, 1987, note 4 pp 7-9). This distinction raises issues about the validity of evidence about a subject's personal history, as against its meaning for them and their perception of it. This is a central issue, concerning the interpretation of that evidence and the priority of the actor's interpretation as against that of the researcher. This also links up directly with black and feminist and neo-Marxist concerns about understanding people's lives, and taking account of ideologies - looking at *both* objective and subjective factors at personal and social levels.

The tradition of life history research has always placed emphasis upon the nature of the research interview as a dialogue, in a sense between two cultures - closely related to anthropologists' concerns about the same issue, (see Gluck, and Patai, 1991). When social divisions are taken fully into account it is not simply a question of 'A good life story' being 'one in which the interviewee takes over control of the interview situation and talks freely' (Bertaux, 1987, p.39), it is much more complex. The relevant concept of 'dialogue' is one which Friere pointed out some time ago is one which should involve a *mutual* attempt not merely to listen to each other's story, but firstly, to come to some appreciation of the principles of interpretation that each other is using, and secondly, to attempt to reach some agreement about the principles that should be used in the light of a mutual awareness of the impact of dominating social groups on the language and concepts that are available, (Freire, 1972). However, it must not be assumed that the researcher is a member of a dominant group - this has to be part of the analysis. There is also now a substantial feminist sociological literature (see numerous references in Stanley, 1990) on the *process* of research which can be closely linked to traditional life history concerns. Older life history studies were not as aware of the implications of the social divisions for their work as they might have been. The issues of power arising from social divisions exists in various combinations on *both* sides of the interview situation, as well as being an integral part of a researcher's institutional position. However the concept of a 'critical life history' approach can explicitly include these dimensions.

The field of *life-course sociology* appears to be of growing importance for understanding personal and family history. As a field of study it can use both the life history method *and* other methods of research in order to understand the interactions between personal and family life-courses and social history. Morgan drew attention to its significance a few years ago when he noted that: 'The 'life course' approach, to date, seems to be the main area where the meeting between history and sociology has made some kind of theoretical contribution', (Morgan, 1985, p.176). It seems to me that it is crucial that a life course approach to understanding people's lives should be an integral part of a 'critical life histories' approach to research.

The essence of life-course sociology is that it places change and development at the centre of the analysis of personal and family lives, and makes connections between 'family time', 'individual time', and historical time'. It is to do with: 'complex relationships over time between ageing, between family, education and work careers, and between historical experiences', (Morgan, 1985, p.177). It is a theoretical improvement over the common approach to family and developmental histories of using 'stages' or 'family cycles' as concepts around which any given family analysis must be organised, and it is in a better position to make connections between biological and psychological time on the one hand, and sociological and historical time on the other. For instance, life-course sociologists have been more appreciative of differences and variation, and concerned with linking historical time with individual biography, rather than the tendency of the life-cycle approach which inteprets family life through the lens of the stereotypical stages of parenthood, 'treating less frequent cases as marginal or deviant', (Morgan, *ibid* p.178). The latter approach has obviously negative implications for understanding gay or lesbian, step-parent, extended households or one-parent 'families'.

Some important aspects of life-course sociology are about the variety of connections that can be made between the different elements. Firstly, there is the issue of the timing and synchronization of life transitions, as between the various individuals, and the family and its sub-groups, with an interactive impact of one on another when individual and 'family' transitions do or do not coincide. Secondly, there is the impact of historical processes such as war or unemployment on the timing of personal and family transitions. This is sometimes accessed by studying comparative cohorts born at different points in time, and can also take in the differential impact of such events and processes on social divisions as they affect the life course (eg Harevan, 1978). Thirdly the concept of 'transition' as used in life-course sociology is broader than that of 'stage', including the idea that any transition has dynamic implications for wider social networks and institutional change. Fourthly, the 'family unit' is unpacked as 'a set of contingent career lines which vary in synchronization and problems of resource management' (Elder, 1978, pp.55-6), whilst retaining the concept of the 'family' as a social system which also has transitions which reciprocally impact on individuals. Fifthly, a life course analysis can focus on either the individual or the 'family' or on other social groups, institutions or informal networks, so it therefore has considerable flexibility and analytical power. For instance, it facilitates the study of *both* the particular life-course of a woman, with its distinctive patterns and transitions, *and* the same life course as part of the life course of a 'family' group and its 'systemic' relationships through time.

Morgan's conclusion makes a point that explicitly links up life-course sociology with the concerns of this paper with anti-oppressive social research: 'this historical approach to the family may show us the interplay between home and work and between the public and the private spheres, thus providing us with some useful linkages with some feminist concerns', (Morgan, 1985, p.179). Indeed, the concept has been put into good use by feminists to illuminate the changing life courses of women and how significantly different they are from those of men, (see Burgoyne, 1987, and Allat, 1987). If black feminist perspectives are about 'relations between history and biography in society' in a way that takes account of power structures and social divisions, then the contribution of both life history as a sociological research methodology, and of life course sociology, is surely of considerable potential significance in contributing to these aims.

Of all the disciplines being used to provide a substantive contribution to 'critical life histories' based on the values of black feminists, the discipline of psychology is the one that has been most criticised by feminists and others for its failure to place itself within social and historical contexts generally, and specifically for its historic inability to come to terms with power and gender issues, (Sherif, 1987). One recent feminist study argues for the importance of black and third world women as clear exemplars of 'associative feminist challenges to psychology's disciplinary boundaries', because such women 'connect psychological variables.. to specific social, political and economic oppressions', (Squires, 1989, pp 116-7). It is significant that Squires identifies the way in which these authors present 'women's subjectivities synecdochally, as a crystallisation of all the social and historical relations that impinge on them', (Squires, *Ibid*, p.119). This links up directly with the concerns of this paper for social research to be made in the light of socially and historically specific relations of power and dominance, so that psychological interpretations of development across the life span must be placed within this context, and not presented as part of a self-contained 'expert' discipline. A recent study of researching psychotherapeutic relationships reaches a similar conclusion: 'an understanding of the synchronic and diachronic features of that relationship's social context must be pursued, drawing upon bodies of knowledge outside of psychology', (Pilgrim, 1990).

The contribution of life-span developmental psychology should therefore be viewed as making a potential contribution to an anti-oppressive perspective on social research, but necessarily one which needs to be re-interpreted systematically in the light of specific historically structured contexts relating to the social divisions. A good example of the necessity of this critique is provided by Gilligan's discussion of Erikson's eight stages of psycho-social development, (Gilligan, 1987). Erikson not only provided a foundation for life-span developmental psychology, but also for psycho-historical studies (Erikson, 1958; 1975; 1977). He is aware of the complex relationship between psychology and history, but he is not able to conceptualise this relationship adequately in terms of the social divisons. Gilligan notes that all his psycho-histories are of 'important' male figures, and his limited awareness of the ill fit of females into his psycho-social stages does not lead to any changes in his idea of development. This remains a conception that is based on the achievement of separation, with female connectedness and attachments being regarded as developmental impediments. Both Erikson and Gilligan have been criticized for basing their work on white populations (Collins 1990).

Although there remain serious and unresolved issues about the nature of child development, there is growing evidence of the significance of childhood experiences as having implications for later stages of development: 'The argument is not that early childhood experiences have no effect, but that the effects of such experiences are mediated by intervening experiences and contingencies, and that personality and behaviour are continually shaped throughout the life cycle', (Runyan, 1988, p.226). There is a clear implication here that a critical life history approach to understanding people's lives should now be an essential part of contemporary psychological developmental theory. This is not only in the sense of putting their behaviour in the context of their own individual and family history, but also placing these within the context of wider structures: 'Particular life-course patterns depend not only on the individual's distinctive interactional styles, but also on the structure of the environment in any given historical period', (Caspi, 1990, p.32).

A further contribution which life span developmental psychology can make towards an anti-oppressive and black feminist framework for social assessment is in the area of understanding the *process* of recalling and recounting personal and family life histories and events. Firstly, there is the way that autobiographical memory changes across the life course, and associated with this, the issue of the construction and validity of personal memory. Secondly, there is the significance of the narrative form as the structure of autobiographical recall and recounting. Thirdly, there is the function of autobiographical memory as an integrating factor for personal identity.

It is not surprising to find that the story a person tells about their own life does not remain static, but changes over time, and clearly this must be taken into account whenever someone is being interviewed about it: 'At any one point in the life course the personal narrative represents a particular interpretation experienced as internally consistent, of currently experienced memories', (Cohler, 1982, p.212). Time itself is experienced differently across the life course, and life span developmental psychology helps to examine these changes. For Cohler, (1982), the overall picture is that the 'developmental organisers of childhood are principally determined by maturation', whilst 'developmental shifts across adulthood are more likely due to socially determined factors' and 'take place in a particular historical context and must be understood as multidirectional', (Cohler, 1982, pp 220-1). In old age there is an increase in reminiscence activity related to the need to reflect upon and integrate perceptions of the past.

In both psychology and history, there is an insistence on the importance of the internal subjective validity of the narrative produced, with respect to its meaning for the individual or group. However, even if it is accepted that there must be elements of myth in all constructions of autobigraphical memory, it would appear to be the case that personal memory is surprisingly effective. One historian, for example, finds that although myths of step-parents help to shape the memories of step-children, 'Time and again real personal experience breaks through, at times negating the myth, ...and giving its own substance to every life story', (Burchardt, 1990). A recent survey of psychological evidence on autobiographical memory tends to confirm this view: 'findings.. suggest that the emotional intensity and personal significance of an event give rise to autobiographical memories which are detailed, highly available for recall, and comparatively resistant to forgetting', (Conway, 1990, p. 104), and that vivid memories in particular, are remarkably consistent over time, (p.87). This even applies to early childhood when according to Freud such emotionally charged memories should be repressed or screened, (p.146).

However, both historians and psychologists agree that even where mythical elements play a part in the construction of autobiographical memory, that does not reduce the importance of the account. From an historical perspective the mythical elements '..need to be seen both as evidence of the past, and as a continuing historical force in the present', (Samuel, and Thompson, 1990, p.20), whilst for the psychologist, '..a defining feature of autobiographical memories was that they inherently represent personal meanings for a specific individual', (Conway, 1990, p.186), and are therefore an important part of that person's identity. Neither is there any need to choose between myth and reality: 'Oral memory offers a double validity in understanding a past in which, as still today, myth was embedded in real experience: both growing from it, and helping to shape its perception', (Samuel, and Thompson, 1990, p.6). This approach is well exemplified before these words were ever written by the black lesbian autobiography of Audre Lorde, which she specifically describes as a 'bio-*myth*ography' in order to stress the point that her writing about herself consciously combines myth and reality in the struggle to be true to her present self and her past, (Lorde, 1984).

Life span developmental psychology and some related areas such as psycho-history and the psychology of memory, can thus be used to further support the concept of a 'critical life history' approach to social research, by giving it the possibility of a psychological dimension which is compatible with anti-oppressive values. However, these disciplines clearly need to be contextualised within the sociological and historical frameworks already discussed for it to be fully consistent with an anti-oppressive methodology.

Critical life histories

The two following diagrams attempt to summarise in an accessible way some of the main points that have been made and need to be considered in a critical life histories approach to research. Diagram 1 is a summary of the contributions of the three disciplines, emphasizing their overlapping perspectives in the context of the lives of the researcher(s) and the subject(s) of research. Diagram 2 attempts to elaborate the implications of this approach for a notional 'family' of 2 adults and a child. In this diagram I have not made clear who is the subject of research - it could be any of the three individuals, or all of them or any combination of the three, depending on the purpose of the research. The point is that this is a micro-study according to critical life history principles.

In diagram 2 there is no reason why the 'family' cannot consist of any variation that matches its multiform realities, including a membership of one. Thus the adults in this example could be gay or lesbian, or heterosexual. What matters is the (contextualised) interaction of various life courses - and this may be more important between people who are not co-habiting at all, although for most people some kind of co-habiting 'family', as well as extended family and relations, will be of crucial importance at various points in their life course. The psychology of individual and group development, as well as that of the research relationship is here systematically placed in social divisions, historical and 'political' contexts. What is not shown - and could not be shown - on this diagram are the actual, multitudinous details which would reflect the multi-layered lives of real historical people. Whilst (I would argue) this methodology is essential to grasp the complex realities of individual members of dominated groups, it will also throw a revealing light on those from dominating groups, because of its systematic and historically contextualised connection of the personal and the political.

114

A framework for anti-oppressive research: Critical life histories   Diagram 1

Life courses of subject(s), starting at date of birth, finishing at death, or at present

Extended family/social networks
•••••••••••••••••••••••••••••

Life course of observer (and agency)

TIME: (viewed chronologically with appropriate dating)   present time

ORAL HISTORY

1 Historical (diachronous) events: the influence of events over other events that follow in time.

2 Synchronous events - mutual interaction at the same point in time, in relation to social and historical power structures. As recalled by subject(s) and in historical documents.

SOCIOLOGY OF THE LIFE COURSE

The social divisions and the social systems which have to be researched, both historically (horizontally) and synchronically (vertically).

Social class
Gender
'Race'
Age
Sexuality
Disability
Others

LIFESPAN DEVELOPMENTAL PSYCHOLOGY

1 Psychological development of individuals and 'family' groups, in relation to their membership of social divisions, throughout their lifespans.

2 Psychological interactions between individuals and group members at specific points in time - in context of historical circumstance and social divisions.

3 Psychology of subject/researcher relationship, given the above contexts.

Individuals, including observer as well as subject.
Cohabitees, relatives
Friends, social networks
Local communities, peer groups
Agencies and institutions, local and national,
    including observer's agency/institution
Social groups and society, regional and national
International connections at individual, group and
    national levels

115

A framework for anti-oppressive research:
Critical life histories - a 2 parent, 1 child family

Diagram 2

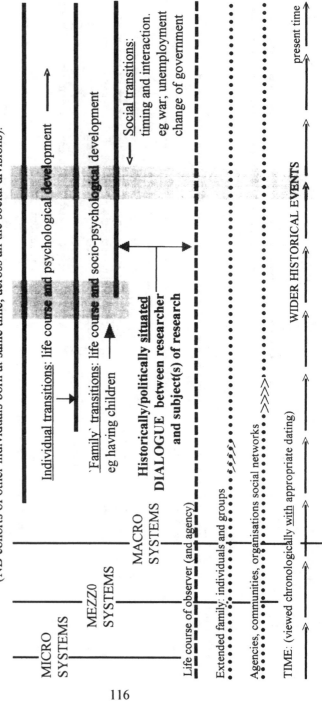

Life courses of subject(s), starting at date of birth, finishing at death, or at present and (self-)identified according to their membership of social divisions, as far as possible. (NB cohorts of other individuals born at same time, across all the social divisions).

<u>Individual transitions</u>: life course and psychological development ———➤

'Family' transitions: life course and socio-psychological development

eg having children

<u>Social transitions</u>:
timing and interaction.
eg war; unemployment
change of government

**Historically/politically situated
DIALOGUE between researcher
and subject(s) of research**

MICRO
SYSTEMS

MEZZO
SYSTEMS

MACRO
SYSTEMS

Life course of observer (and agency)

Extended family: individuals and groups

Agencies, communities, organisations social networks

TIME: (viewed chronologically with appropriate dating)

WIDER HISTORICAL EVENTS

present time

116

In diagram 2 I have separated out social, 'family' and individual transitions. In practice, of course, they overlap, and may have similar causes. The suggested example of child birth is obviously an individual transition for those concerned - in very different ways - as well as a 'family' transition for the group as a whole. Social transitions will impact on individuals and families in both direct and indirect ways, depending on the social divisions involved. A matter of particular interest is the relationship between a member of an oppressed group; other members of that group at all social levels, and what is happening in the wider society, locally and nationally. A good example of this is given in Morley and Stanley's study of Emily Wilding Davison, (Morley and Stanley, 1988). A particular event, such as the expulsion of Kenyan Asians, will have immediate impact on the lives of black people involved directly, (perhaps they or their kin are involved), or indirectly because of the outburst of racism that followed, whilst white people will receive or participate in the media coverage of the event.

The methodology thus directs researchers to make connections between the personal and the political at all levels including themselves. The main elements of this research method are:

1.   The study of the life courses of people, groups and organisations from a
     'critical' perspective - one which is explicitly based on anti-oppressive
     values. This is not only a matter of having a basis of ethical and
     political values with which to judge the relevance of various factors or the
     appropriateness of different courses of action. It is also a matter of a
     specific methodology of doing life histories: it is not merely 'life history' as
     traditionally studied - with the values added on. It means the systematic
     examination of all the aspects of the research in terms of all the social
     divisions.
2.   The study of life courses from a multi-disciplinary perspective: one which is
     not the result of an eclectic selection of techniques, but which is oriented
     towards the consistent realisation of a methodology which reflects anti-
     oppressive values. The concept of a multi-disciplinary approach is in itself
     essential to such a value base, where understanding oppression in people's
     lives has to be multi-layered and complex.
3.   The use of an historical approach to the understanding of lives, which
     places them in a series of simultaneous historical contexts at micro, mezzo
     and macro levels. The study of historical change within the different but
     related time frames - personal and social, using oral history techniques to
     access the richness and detail of people's lives; their perceptions of and

'myths' concerning their own life stories. The study of personal and public historical documents that can supplement and complement the views of the historical actors.

4. The use of sociological techniques for understanding the place of a life within the social structure, and particularly, the concept of the life course, and its flexible orientation to the variety of concerns that an anti-oppressive methodology demands in the study of people's lives. For example, the importance of being able to focus simultaneously on the specific life-course patterns associated with an individual's place within the social power structure, *and* the life course of households and other organisations and institutions with which the individual also shares a life, and which interacts over time with theirs.

5. The study of the psychological life-span in the context of the historical and sociological factors associated with the social divisions. The interpretation of the actors' perceptions, and their psychological self concept and social identity only in the light of such a socially and historically situated psychology, and its interaction with that of the researcher.

6. The simultaneous study of the biography of the researcher as it comes into connection with the life courses being studied, and of the politics, psychology and ethics of this structured relationship, and the relative 'knowledge' that this process produces. In particular it involves a careful analysis of, and sensitivity to, the power issues that influence the process and outcomes. These will arise principally from the major social divisions, but will overlap with other structures such as the research relationship and its particular institutional setting.

The 'critical life history' approach to social research is a subset of critical approaches to social research, some of which are described in Harvey, (1990). In his terms I am drawing on 'critical ethnography' and 'radical historicism', but with *specific* sociological, historical and psychological methodologies to support an anti-oppressive approach to understanding people's lives that is particularly relevant to professionals and practitioners in the social, health and welfare fields, where it is important to be able to understand micro (and mezzo) level social phenomena in their particularity, without sacrificing anything to the fundamental structuring of such phenomena by social divisions, including considerations that arise even from international divisions and relationships. The usefulness of such an approach will cover a variety of practical situations, throwing light on individual lives, groups, organisations, institutions and communities.

The 'critical life histories' approach does not need to be understood in purely 'subjective' or qualitative terms - whatever these terms are taken to mean. A recent collection of sociological papers illustrates the point:

> Another extremely important development which is taking place is the attempt to integrate qualitative and quantitative research on life and work histories. (Dex, 1991, p.3.).

The validity of personal life histories can be checked against personal and public documents, and their stories can be compared also with other related life stories. They may be chosen as representative of a social group, or can be interviewed as being of interest for their own sake, depending on the particular purpose of the research. There is every reason to 'triangulate' critical life history research with other qualitative and quantitative approaches, but it can also stand on its own as a valuable resource which is cost effective as well as anti-oppressive.

References

Allat, A. (1987), *Women and the Life Cycle*, London: Routledge.

Bertaux, D. (ed) (1981), `Biography and Society: The Life History Approach in the Social Sciences*, California: Sage.

Bhavnani, K-K, (1990),'What's power got to do with it? Empowerment and social research', in Parker, I. and Shotter, J. (eds) *Deconstructing Social Psychology*, London: Routledge.

Borland, K. (1991), "That's not what I said": interpretative conflict in oral narrative research, in Gluck, S.B. and Patai, D. (eds) *Women's Words*.

Bryan, B., Dadzie, S.and Scarfe, S. (1985), *The Heart of the Race: Black Women's Lives in Britain*, London: Virago.

Burchardt, N. (1990), 'Stepchildren's memories', in Samuel, R. and Thompson, P. (eds) (1990) *The Myths We Live By*, London: Routledge.

Burgoyne, J. (1987),'Change. gender and the life course', in Cohen, G.(ed) *Social Change and the Life Course*, London: Tavistock.

Caspi, H., Elder, G.H. and Herbener, E.S. (1990), 'Childhood personality and the prediction of life-course pattern', in Robins, L.N. and Rutter, M.(eds) *Straight and Devious Pathways from Childhood to Adulthood*, Cambridge: Cambridge University Press.

Cohler, B.J. (1982), 'Personal narratives and the life course', in Baltes, P.B. and Brim, O.G. (1982) *Life-Span Development and Behaviour*, Vol 4, New York: Academic Press.

Collins, P.H. (1990), *Black Feminist Thought*, London: Unwin.

Conway, M.A. (1990), *Autobiographical Memory*, Milton Keynes: Open University Press.

Davis, A. (1982), *Women, Race and Class*, London: The Women's Press.

Davis, A. (1989), *Women, Culture and Politics*, London: The Women's Press.

Dex, S. (ed) (1991), *Life and Work History Analyses: Qualitative and Quantitative Developments*, London: Routledge.

Elder, G.H.Jnr, (1978), 'Family history and the life course', in Harevan, T.K., (ed) *op. cit.*

Erikson, E. (1958), *Young Man Luther: A Study in Psychoanalysis and History*, New York: Norton.

Erikson, E. (1975), *Life history and the Historical Moment*, New York: Norton.

Erikson, E. (1977), *Childhood and Society*, St Albans: Triad/Paladin.

Etter-Lewis, G. (1991), 'Black women's life stories: reclaiming self in narrative texts', in Gluck, S.B. and Patai, D.

Freire, P. (1972) *Pedagogy of the Oppressed*, London: Sheed and Ward.

Gluck, S.B. and Patai, D. (1991), *Women's Words: The Feminist Practice of Oral History*, London: Routledge.

Gilligan, C. (1987), 'Women's place in man's life cycle', in Harding, S. *Feminism and Methodology*, Milton Keynes: Open University Press.

Harevan, T.K. (ed) (1978), *Transitions; The Family and the Life Course in Historical Perspective*, New York: Academic Press.

Harvey, L. (1990), *Critical Social Research*, London: Unwin Hyman.

Hooks, B. (1982), *Ain't I a Woman?: Black Women and Feminism*, London: Pluto Press.

Hooks, B. (1984), *Feminist Theory: From Margin to Center*, Boston: South End Press.

Hooks, B. (1989), *Talking Back. Thinking Feminist, Thinking Black*, London: Sheba Feminist Publishers.

Jordan, J. (1989), *Moving Towards Home. Political Essays*, London: Virago.

Lorde, A. (1982), *ZAMI, A New Spelling of My Name*, London: Sheba Feminist Publishers.

Lorde, A. (1984), *Sister Outsider*, New York: The Crossing Press.

Lorde, A. (1988), *A Burst of Light*, London: Sheba Feminist Publishers.

Mama, A.(1989), *The Hidden Struggle*, London: London Race and Housing Research Unit.

Mbilinyi, M. (1989), '"I'd have been a man": politics and the labour process in producing personal narratives', in Personal Narratives Group, *Interpreting Women's Lives, op.cit.*

Morgan, D.H.J. (1985), *The Family: Politics and Social Theory*, London: Routledge.

Morley, Ann, with Stanley, L. (1988), *The Life and Death of Emily Wilding Davison*, London: The Women's Press.

Olsen, K. and Shopes, L. (1991), 'Crossing boundaries, building bridges', in Gluck, S.B. and Patai, D. (eds) *Women's Words, op.cit.*

Parkes, M.,Stevenson-Hinde , J. and Marris, P. (eds) (1991), *Attachment Across the Life Cycle*, London: Routledge.

Parma, P. (1990), 'Black feminism: the politics of articulation', in Rutherford, J.(ed) *Identity, Community, Culture, Difference*, London: Lawrence and Wishart.

121

Personal Narratives Group, (eds) (1989), *Interpreting Women's Lives: Feminist Theory and Personal Narratives*, Bloomington: Indiana University Press.

Pilgrim, D. (1990), 'Researching psychotherapy in Britain: the limits of a psychological approach', in Parker, I. and Shotter, J. (eds) *Deconstructing Social Psychology*, London: Routledge.

Plummer, K. (1983), *Documents of Life: An Introduction to the Problems and Literature of a Humanistic Method*, London: Unwin Hyman.

Runyan, W.M. (1988), *Psychology and Historical Interpretation*, Oxford: Oxford University Press.

Samuel, R. and Thompson, P. (eds) (1990), *The Myths We Live By*, London: Routledge.

Sherif, C. (1987), 'Bias in psychology', in Harding, S. *Feminism and Methodology*, Milton Keynes: Open University Press.

Squires, C. (1989), *Significant Differences - Feminism in Psychology*, London: Routledge.

Stacey, J. (1991), 'Can there be a feminist ethnography?', in Gluck, S.B. and Patai, D. (eds) *Women's Words, op.cit.*

Stanley, L. (1987), 'Biography as microscope or kaleidoscope? The case of 'power' in Hannah Cullwick's relationship with Arthur Munby' *Women's Studies International Forum*, 10: 1, pp.19-31.

Stanley, L. (ed) (1990), *Feminist Praxis*, London: Routledge.

Thompson, P. (1984) (2nd Ed), *The Voice of the Past*, London: Routledge.

Williams, F. (1989) , *Social Policy: A Critical Introduction*, Cambridge: Polity Press.

122

7 Developing a feminist participative research framework: Evaluating the process

Marion Martin

Research can serve either to reinforce oppressive structures and relationships or it can serve to challenge these (Field, 1991). The research study that provides the focus for discussion in this chapter set out to make a contribution to those studies that have sought to challenge oppression and oppressive structures. That is to say an attempt was made to develop an anti-oppressive research strategy within the context of a small community-based case study. The size of the study in terms of population is not the primary issue here, rather the focus is on the particular *research process* developed. In the discussion that follows I take the position that feminist and participative research approaches provide particularly appropriate means of developing anti-oppressive research. There is of course nothing new in such a claim. However, in my experience it is considerably easier to discuss the advantages and potential of these research approaches in a theoretical sense than it is to actually carry them out. The major aims of this chapter therefore are to describe how the research was designed and carried out informed by a feminist/participative framework; to evaluate the research process in terms of the participative dimension; to comment on some of the difficulties I encountered as a researcher working within this paradigm framework. The discussion raises a number of issues about research as an imperfect process drawing attention to the myriad factors in the research context that mitigate against participation and empowerment. This is not to deny the validity of feminist participative research (FPR) as an anti-oppressive research approach that has an important contribution to make to broader liberation struggles but it does provide an opportunity to consider some of the complexities, perhaps particularly for professionals, in learning to work *with* people rather than *on* or *for* people.

123

Before moving on to look at the actual research context it is important to consider more closely the claim that FPR approaches are particularly appropriate in challenging oppressive structures. In order to do this I think it is helpful to briefly examine the concept of the research paradigm. A paradigm is essentially a way of viewing or making sense of the world from a particular value position. Clearly the value position we hold as researchers for instance, influences the topics we seek to research, the kind of knowledge we seek to generate and the way we go about actually doing the research ie the methodology adopted.

Among major research paradigms which have been identified in the context of the social sciences are *positivist, ethnographic, participative and feminist.* The positivist and ethnographic paradigms are placed under the category of *traditional* paradigms. In a sense this is strange as at first glance these two paradigms seem to represent opposite value positions in that the positivist paradigm assumes objectivity and detachment of the researcher in the research process; emphasis is placed on the collection and analysis of data in numerical form and much of the value base of this paradigm emerges from its roots in the dominant scientific paradigm. The ethnographic paradigm on the other hand, seeks to develop an inductive research process placing value on inter-subjective, qualitative research methods reaching towards involvement and seeking to engage the holistic qualities of the research context (Humphries 1994). However, while arising from what could be described as opposite poles with regard to their philosophical origins these paradigms hold two important characteristics in common. The first is that both are *vertical* or *imposing* in approach. That is to say, the control of the research process - topic, method, interpretation - is held by the researcher. In this sense the research design can be said to be *imposed* from above *onto* individuals or groups. In line with this the research process has an *extractive* quality in that knowledge generated from research is generally taken out of the research context rather than fed back into the ongoing life situation of the researched and towards the development of all those involved in the research process (Maguire 1987).

It was partly in response to a growing awareness of the inappropriateness of traditional paradigms as a science of people that the alternative participative and feminist paradigms emerged in the 1970's (Hall 1992). In the early stages of the development of participative research (PR) Hall, a leading practitioner in this field defined PR as:

... a three-pronged activity ...a method of social investigation involving the full participation of the community... an educational process which is a means of taking action for development. (Hall 1977:1).

The key words in this definition are *participation, education* and *action*. Thus PR is a three part process of social inquiry and learning for *both* researcher and researched which results in action being taken on the original need, problem or issue identified in the initial stages of the research process. Maguire writes:

Rather than merely recording observable facts, participatory research has the explicit intention of collectively investigating reality in order to transform it. (Maguire 1987:3).

Hall (1977) identifies various components of PR, four of which are outlined here. First, the *need or problem* on which the research is focused *originates within the community* which is the SUBJECT of the research process. The research problem is defined and data collected and analyzed and the problem 'solved' in and by the community. Secondly, *PR seeks to involve groups who have been marginalised in society* and who have been, through various means and for various reasons, denied power. Thirdly, it *recognizes the strength and power such groups already have and seeks to build on this* through the research process thus making research an integral part of community development. PR sets out to reduce the power held by the researcher and give back power to the subjects of research. Central to this approach is the need for *the researcher to be a committed participant and learner* in the research process. This leads to a *committed involvement* rather than detachment.

Given this value base it is difficult to accept that PR has acted from a largely androcentric (male bias) position for so many years. Maguire (1987) makes the point that it was not until 1981 that Hall raised the question: 'How can PR be human centred, not man-centred?' (Hall 1981, p17)

This debate continues today among members of both PR and feminist communities (Maguire 1987). The feminist paradigm has arisen as part of this debate and stands alongside PR within the alternative paradigm framework. Many feminists propose changes that reflect the diversity of BOTH female and male realities in the theory and practice of research. Humphries (1994) identifies the following as assumptions within the feminist paradigm that:

125

- The experiences of women are often distorted or made invisible in research, whether positivist, ethnographic or participative.

- Feminist research (FR) is premised on the oppression of women and committed to changing it.

- The researcher's experience as a woman should allow for a less exploitative relationship between the researcher and researched than is the case in other paradigms.

However, FR does not consist of a set of agreed guidelines and methods. Nor is there a clear definition of FR rather there is a continued dialogue as to whether or not it is appropriate to agree a definition which will bring feminists together rather than divide them (Coyner & Brooks 1986).

There are no unanimously agreed answers but feminist literature shows that various approaches called FR have evolved and overall these share certain characteristics some of which have been outlined above. (See also for examples Stanley and Wise 1983, Bowles and Klein 1983, Mohanty 1991).

An important aspect of the debates around FR is the critique of FR in the *first world* by some of the many women struggling against oppressive forces in *third world* contexts.

In her article 'Under Western Eyes' Chandra Mohanty (1991) maintains that much of the discourse in the rapidly growing field of 'women and development' arises from western feminists the majority of whom present an homogeneous view of the 'average third world woman' as essentially uneducated, poor, tradition-bound and victimized. In contrast, the first world woman is taken to be educated, able to take control of her life and 'modern' in her attitudes and approaches to living. Mohanty refers to western feminists who hold such views as 'imperialist feminists'. She makes the point that many third world women have a long tradition of the search for social justice, freedom and equality (See also Felizio 1992, Shiva 1990) yet these struggles and histories remain unacknowledged by many western feminists. In such contexts western feminisms may be as *vertical* and *imposing* in approach as the traditional positivist or ethnographic paradigms.

Thus feminist research encompasses an enormous variety of need and experience. As with all grass roots inquiry,organisation and action, FR should be expressed in its own particular, localised historical, political and socio-economic context.

It is of course possible to think in one paradigm position, yet to practice within another. This is not uncommon. In part this is due to a dual consciousness regarding understanding of reality (Mies 1983). It may also be due to significant external factors that influence practice such as which paradigm perspectives are most powerful, influential and 'respectable' in the institutional and social networks we live and work within. I find the concept of a *paradigm continuum* helpful as it expresses the potential fluidity or dynamic quality of these different conceptual states of theory and practice. Indeed my own paradigm position has changed since I embarked upon the research that is the focus of discussion here.

The preceding discussion makes it clear that research cannot take place within a vacuum. Research is always a political process. A major concern of the feminist participative researcher (FPR) is to make her ideological bias explicit (Ellis 1990) and to acknowledge the need to recognize the role she plays in the research process (Stanley & Wise 1983).

Against this background and with an awareness of some of these debates this research set out to explore the possibilities for PR informed by feminist perspectives, to avoid some of the pitfalls and exploitative potential discussed above. The following part of this chapter presents a *reflection* on this *process*.

The research context

The research project was carried out within the context of a women's health centre (WHC). The term community is used to describe the WHC in the sense that it is a community of shared needs that has arisen from a wider community, that of a fairly small rural town in the north of England. The centre had been in existence for about 3 years when this research took place. It was supported by a small grant through a central government source but had come into existence from the local community as opposed to being initiated by some external source. Several women had noticed concern among local women that health care particularly at the primary level was not meeting the needs that many women had for appropriate counselling and access to information with regard to a range of issues related to bereavement, stress, depression, sexuality and family planning, side effects of anti-depressant or tranquilliser treatment (Graham 1993). Eventually, with the support of the local Community Health Council and various public meetings the WHC was set up. It was situated in a small flat in an easily accessible part of the town near the main shopping area. The Centre was staffed by a part time co-ordinator and a number of volunteer workers. The overall aim of the Centre was to provide a local service working towards health promotion through access to relevant health related information. The Centre aimed to move towards meeting this broad aim by providing a variety of services mainly through its volunteers all of whom were experienced women some of whom were also health professionals, though the latter were a minority. Services provided included counselling, self-help groups, health studies courses, an information base regarding health issues along with information about local health resources both conventional and alternative. Information was also disseminated through health days and workshops with other local community groups.

Before negotiating access to this community I had spent time considering an appropriate methodology for the research. I was concerned that the research should have a feminist orientation and that it should be informed by the participative paradigm. During the course of reading I came across the writings of Shulamitz Reinharz (1983). Reinharz has developed a participative research model she calls 'experiential analysis'. In this model she identifies two qualities that need to be present if the research is to be participative. Firstly, the research focus (areas of inquiry) must be of sincere interest to *both* researcher and researched as feminist participative research is particularly dependant on co-operative relationships. Secondly, the research outcome should be relevant and immediately applicable to the everyday problems, interests, needs of the subjects of research. Reinharz maintains that when the above two qualities are present a co-operative and trusting relationship is more likely to be established between researched and researcher.

In order to facilitate the growth of this relationship Reinharz maintains that the researcher must be 'seen about' the organisation/situation that is the focus of research. This provides not only the researcher but also the subjects of research with the opportunity to assess one another from first hand contact. This is important because:

One's trustworthiness is not confined to what one says...but also to how one acts and who one is. (Reinharz 1983:177).

In this situation the power imbalance between the researcher and subjects of research is, to some degree, balanced by the explicit acknowledgement between the parties involved of their shared roles as participant observers. While the researcher observes, she is also being observed. This is a point that is rarely alluded to or discussed in most research accounts.

Reinharz holds that feminist research within a participative framework should take place within the 'natural setting' of the subjects of the research, whether this is within the organisational 'home' of the subjects or within the homes of individuals or groups. This provides the researcher with the opportunity to become involved in the everyday environment of the researched. Within this setting the researcher is given the opportunity to see and experience the various ways in which people interact with the researcher and with one another. The researcher is thus more able to take a background rather than a foreground role because she '...is not manipulating the environment but is part of it'(Reinharz 1983:178). In this way data gathered in the 'natural setting' reflects, to whatever degree it can accurately reflect, people being in situations to which they give meaning and which 'shapes their making of themselves and meaning' (Reinharz 1983:178). In approaching the research I tried to ensure that all these dimensions - a common interest, relevance and applicability, shared roles, involvement of the researcher in everyday activities - informed decisions at every stage.

The research design and process

The purpose of this section of the chapter is to describe the research process on a step by step basis. I hope this will not prove too tedious but it is this close examination of process that is so rarely given the detailed attention it requires. As I plan to present an evaluation of the research process with regard to 'measuring' the level of participation achieved, it is necessary to outline the process in some detail. Given the preceding discussion regarding the development of an appropriate theoretical framework for FPR, the question arises as to how far research practice can meet theory? Where do the gaps between theory and practice occur? Why have these gaps developed? Such questions offer a framework with which to critique the research process. As FPR is very much context focused, issues that occur in this particular study cannot necessarily be assumed to occur in other research contexts even though they may share many similarities with this study. Nevertheless, lessons can be learned from an evaluation such as that presented below.

The idea of carrying out research in the area of women organising at community level around health issues occurred to me. At this time a particular interest of mine was in small, localised grassroots women's movements that had developed under the control of local women in response to felt need in the community. This coincided with an opportunity to do a higher degree. Approaching the research from a feminist value base I hoped the research would feed into areas of identified needs in the community and act as a means of unearthing and generating knowledge that could be used in taking appropriate action on the expressed needs of local women. At about this time I met the co-ordinator of a such a group and shared my interest with her. I explained that I would like to carry out a research project with a group like the one she was working with. I hoped it would be possible for both the group and myself to benefit from the research. I explained that I would like the research to focus on areas the group would like to explore further. The cost to the Women's Health Centre (WHC) would be minimum as I would be responsible for finding a means of supporting myself financially while the research was taking place.

The co-ordinator's initial response was one of interest but concern. The interest seemed to stem from the recognition that this was a rare opportunity for the group and they should make use of it. Such research could well be put to use for funding purposes. The concern appeared to lie in a sense of anxiety and feelings of vulnerability at the prospect of 'being researched'. Nevertheless, she took the idea to the group's management team, all of whom were voluntary workers. The team later invited me to meet them so that they could make their own assessment of me and talk through the idea of research. A few days later I was informed that they had decided they were interested and I could base myself at the WHC once timing etc had been negotiated with them. At this preliminary stage of negotiating access I had not found an opportunity to discuss in any detail the research approach I thought it would be appropriate to use. I took the opportunity to do this when I was invited to a second meeting. I explained something of the major concepts of FPR and why I thought it was the most appropriate approach to employ in this context. I explained that this would mean at least a core group of women from the centre would have to be prepared to commit a fair degree of time to working with me on designing the research by identifying aims, methods, collecting data etc. The reaction was one of surprise and some confusion. After all, surely I had been the one to suggest the research and therefore I was the person who should do it! Anyway, research is a specialised process and requires an 'expert'. They knew nothing of research methods or analysis of data. I was seen to be the one who had the time, energy, specialist knowledge and skills. They after all were 'just ordinary women' with their time and energy already at full stretch with family responsibilities, part time and in many cases extremely low paid jobs. In addition they struggled to find time and space for supporting the women's group they had worked so hard to set up. I needed to understand that on top of all this they simply had no time, let alone

130

the skills and confidence to design and then carry out a piece of research. This kind of 'resistance' made a lot of sense! I will return at a later point to a more detailed discussion of some of the issues this threw up. In the end we reached a compromise. An agreement was made that the management group would represent the wider WHC and the research aims would be negotiated between the management group and myself. After considerable discussion the following 7 aims were agreed:

Researcher initiated and community agreed

1. Examine the ideology aims and objectives of the Centre

2. Examine and clarify the nature of the educational processes employed on the health studies courses run at the Centre.

3. Enquire into women's perceptions of their health education needs.

Community initiated and researcher agreed

4. Enquire into women's ('users') perceptions of the purpose of the centre.

5. Enquire into the extent to which the Centre met 'users' health needs.

6. Enquire into the worker group's perceptions of the style of leadership in the Centre.

7. Enquire into local health professionals' attitudes towards and understanding of the purpose of the Centre and their attitudes towards it.

From the aims it can be seen that a major interest of the group was evaluation. As such grassroots groups have little money, energy and time available to put towards evaluation much of their work and efforts go quite unrecognized and unacknowledged. We were united in our concern that this research should result in both public recognition and increased social and financial support for the Centre.

131

Research methods

The selection of the research methods was almost totally given over to my 'expertise as a researcher'. While the research aims had been negotiated and power and control in the research process were fairly well balanced between researcher and community this was not the case in the selection of research methods. There was some discussion of methods and why particular methods might be the most appropriate. Both quantitative and qualitative methods were selected with the emphasis on qualitative as the following indicates:

- Centre documents and literature review.

- Individual Interviews using a semi-structured interview schedule with Centre 'users' and management team.

- Participant observation

- Group interviews with management team and members of self help groups.

- Mailed questionnaires to health professionals.

The interview schedules and all other methods for data collection were designed by me though discussed with most members of the management committee. The one exception was the mailed questionnaires which were to be sent out to the health professionals. Most of the questions were designed collaboratively as this was an area where the group had very clear ideas regarding the information they wanted.

Data collection

Apart from the document and literature review this involved:

- Thirty individual interviews

- Four group meetings

- Participant observation at 8 meetings of the health studies course

- Four group meetings

- Six open Centre meetings

- Fifty five mailed questionnaires

Data collection was completed by me working on my own. Data analysis took place simultaneously with data collection and again this aspect of the research was controlled by me. This was not as collaborative as I desired but it was necessary to compromise or little would be achieved within a participative framework at all.

It was now 7 months into the project. Now the research process began to move towards a more collaborative approach. Following data analysis I wrote a draft report on the findings making it clear this was my interpretation of the findings. I also outlined some recommendations. At the request of the WHC the report was made available to all who had participated in the research to date bar the health professionals. Everyone was given right of comment and a meeting was held for all participants. At the meeting, which was well attended, a few questions were raised about the report and several changes were agreed. By early May these had been incorporated into the final report.

It was now almost 10 months since the idea of the research had arisen. Expenses had not been great for the Centre as I had supported myself throughout and the group had contributed to the research financially by carrying the costs of postage for the mailed questionnaires and the typing and distribution of the final report.

In the earlier discussion concerning the theoretical framework of FPR I emphasised the importance placed on ensuring the research process results in ACTION that builds into the development of the group on its terms. Below, are several of the actions taken as a consequence of the research findings:

- The questionnaire to local health professionals elicited a remarkable 80% response rate. There is no space to discuss the response rate but it was encouraging to the WHC. The questionnaire response made it possible to identify which health professionals were interested in the work of the Centre. A plan was made for members of the Centre to make contact with health professionals who expressed an interest in developing contact. One of the plans was to discuss future collaboration and the appropriate referral of women from the health professionals to the Centre. Among other actions taken were the following:

- An opportunity to explore issues related to group dynamics and leadership styles was set up. Leadership style had emerged as an important issue which it was felt could be explored in a reasonably anonymous way through the research process.

- Fortnightly support meetings were organised for volunteers who worked as individual counsellors. Up to this time no formal support structure had existed. The research helped to identify this unmet need.

-The findings showed evidence of many very positive responses from Centre 'users' about the value of the Centre and its contribution to raising the quality of life of local women such as themselves through providing needed and otherwise often inaccessible information and support. Such findings were used by the Centre in seeking future funding.

- The group set up an internal evaluation of the Centre's work the following year incorporating aspects of the collaborative process.

Towards a framework for evaluation of the research process

One of the problems associated with FPR is its sometimes vague and nebulous quality. This can present an obstacle to researchers and community groups pursuing this research approach and considering it valid. This provides all the more reason for developing a means of evaluating the participative process and identifying its strengths and limitations. John Heron (1981) has suggested that participative research can be placed on a continuum according to the extent that it is predominantly researcher controlled. Heron refers to this side of the continuum as representing the 'traditional' PR model, or BOTH researcher with community controlled. The other side of the continuum represents the 'experiential' PR model. The latter refers to research that is predominantly controlled by the researched.

Hall (1977) has offered a series of questions that can be usefully applied to the research process. I have loosely adapted Hall's evaluation framework for the purpose of evaluating this case study in order to gauge the extent to which the research process lies towards the traditional end of Heron's PR continuum or the experiential end. I do not intend to suggest that the results provide an accurate evaluation but they do offer some clarity to an otherwise complex area of research activity.

In order to place the case study on Heron's continuum an adaptation of Hall's evaluation questions are addressed to the research process. The interpretation given below is my own and does not necessarily reflect the views of the researched. Due to the time that has passed since the research was carried out it has not been realistic to involve the WHC workers in this evaluation.

Evaluation framework

1. Initiation and control

a) Who initiated the research?

The research was initiated by the researcher and following negotiation it was finally agreed to by a core group of centre workers who put themselves forward as representatives of the WHC. The initiation process was thus primarily researcher controlled.

b) Who defined the problem or the aims of the research?

Both researcher and community were involved in this process. The researcher initiated 3 aims and the community agreed to these while the community initiated 4 aims and the researcher agreed to these. Thus both researcher and community shared control of the research process to some degree at this stage.

c) Who paid for the research?

This is always a crucial question and in many contexts the group/agency who pay hold the control. In this instance this was a relatively small piece of research which was internally financed. This created both constraints with regard to the size of the project but it also allowed for more flexibility and negotiation. In fact the financial costs were shared fairly equally between the researcher who gave her time etc freely and the community who took responsibility for the costs of the mailed questionnaires, typing up the draft and final research reports and disseminating these.

2. Critical content

a) Who decides what is studied?
This, as b) above indicates, was shared between researcher and community.

b) By whom is it studied?
This aspect of the research was primarily researcher controlled as the community felt they had not sufficient time, confidence, knowledge or skill to complete this aspect of the study that required the ability to select appropriate research methods to gather information in relation to the various aims.

c) By whom was it studied?
This aspect of the research was controlled by the researcher for the same reasons given in a) above.

3. Collective analysis

a) Who gathers information?
Information was gathered entirely by the researcher, so this aspect of the research was researcher controlled and more closely akin to traditional research approaches.

b) Who analyzes the data?
The data was analyzed by the researcher.

4. Learning and skills

a) *What learning has taken place? What skills have been developed and by whom?*

Both researcher and community members have increased their information and confidence base with regard to research activities. Though the extent to which individuals have learned will probably be related to the extent to which they have been or have felt able to participate in the research process. For the researcher participatory research skills have been learnt such as negotiating aims of the project,research methods, skills in individual and group interviewing etc. Some community members have developed insight into the ways decisions are made in

136

the centre, clearer insight is gained as to how the centre wants leadership to operate, how they might usefully build relationships with various interested health professionals and how a future evaluation might be carried out using a participative approach. The educational aspect of the research process is thus shared by both researcher and community members to varying degrees.

5. Uses of research for action

a) Who decides how and where research results are disseminated?
This was primarily decided by the community though there was some negotiation with the researcher.

b) Who uses the results?
Findings were used by both researcher and community. By the community primarily for future development of the Centre and for future funding purposes. By the researcher for academic purposes and information dissemination by other routes.

c) Who benefits from the research?
Both researcher and community benefitted for reasons already stated.

The response to the above evaluation framework is converted into numerical form below. The number 1 indicates where the locus of power at any one time is seen to lie.

EVALUATION FRAMEWORK

1. Initiation & control

	Researcher	Community
Who initiates the research?	1	
Who defines the problem?	1	1
Who pays for the research?	1	1

137

2. Critical content

	Researcher	Community
Who decides what is studied	1	1

3. Collective analysis

Who gathers the data?	1	
Who analyses the data?	1	

4. Learning and skills developed?

Who has developed increased information base and confidence base?	1	1

5. Uses for action

Who decides how the results will be disseminated?	1	1
Who uses the research findings?	1	1
Who benefits from the research?	1	1
TOTAL	10	7

Using this evaluation framework it can be seen that this case study falls into the traditional side of Heron's PR continuum. While this is admittedly a crude measurement of participation it is of some value and can be used as a good basis for discussion for the planning of any such future research. I place the level of participation at the approximate point on the continuum below.

138

PARTICIPATIVE RESEARCH CONTINUUM

Traditional PR Model   Experiential PR Model

1.................**....5O......................1OO

Heron makes the point that the majority of PR projects fall closer to the traditional than to the experiential model. I do not see this as a cause for despair for those who believe this approach to research has an important contribution to make to research which challenges oppressive structures. However, the more successful and genuine collaboration can be and the more widespread this can be within the overall community, the more research will be likely to make a contribution to sustained development of the community on its terms rather than those of the researcher or the agency the researcher represents. It becomes clear then that FPR presents a very different research model to that of the traditional positivist and ethnographic research paradigms with their vertical and extractive qualities tending to draw resources and strength FROM community groups rather than building on the strengths that already exist.

Before concluding the chapter it may be helpful to highlight some of the factors that stood in the way of developing a more collaborative research process.

"MIND THE GAP!" - Difficulties Encountered in Doing FPR

(i) Lack of time for overcoming the problem of mystique associated with research.

What inevitably emerges is a gap between theory and practice. Both the Centre workers and I encountered unexpected difficulties as we explored ways of working together. Initially there was a mystique associated with the concept of 'research' and a sense of uneasiness with the prospect of 'being researched'. While FPR seeks to move towards overcoming such fears and barriers, this is not easily done. The situation is further exacerbated by lack of time. While I had anticipated the time problem I was impatient to encourage a collaborative approach to planning, particularly in the early stages. In so doing I was not as

139

sensitive as I might have been. This resulted in a problem also encountered by Eldon (1981):

...in my haste to press on with participatory research I was not too democratic; my actions belied my intentions. (Eldon 1981:255).

(ii) Cultural invasion of researched by researcher

One of the dangers is that the researcher can find herself imposing her values on the researched. The process Freire refers to as 'cultural invasion' (Freire 1972). Thus instead of facilitating co-operation and dialogue there is a tendency to create a relationship of 'anti-dialogue' which may lead to hostility and act in direct opposition to collaborative work. It seems therefore that it is crucial, when adopting this research approach to allow for adequate time for all concerned to develop an understanding of the processes involved and for the researcher to be particularly aware of the effects of her demands on others involved in the research process.

(iii) Rhetoric and reality

Brown and Kaplan (1981) maintain that participative research involves a 'dialectic among the perspectives of diverse parties' (p.311). This point bears some relation to a third difficulty encountered with regard to the nature of the Centre core worker group. I had understood that this group tried to work in a collective manner. Participative research therefore seemed a particularly appropriate research model to adopt as such a group should I assumed, be accustomed to working in a co-operative way. However, I was to discover that while the worker group aimed towards egalitarian relationships there was in fact a marked hierarchy within the group. There was a gap between rhetoric and reality. I had not anticipated this. The existing hierarchy of relationships acted against the collaborative process. This has been a valuable insight. If involved in future research of this kind I would be concerned during the period of preparation to explore and examine group dynamics and individual members perceptions of those dynamics. When people are familiar, as most of us are, in working within hierarchical organisational structures, learning to work in a more egalitarian, co-operative and trusting manner takes time. It involves risk-taking and demands a high degree of personal and collective commitment. It cannot be assumed that these qualities are present or that the organisational environment will 'allow' them to emerge.

(iv) Differences between researched and researcher

The fourth major difficulty encountered relates both to the participative process and the complex nature of the researcher/researched relationship(s). Most of the women involved in the research seemed to see and relate to me in the early stages, as an 'expert', because I was a researcher. I felt ill at ease with this image, partly because I did not see myself as an 'expert' and partly because this view of me served to create a hierarchical relationship (gap) between the other women and myself which I was trying to avoid. My professional qualifications as a nurse and social worker contributed to this situation. The majority of the women I interviewed had little in the way of formal educational qualifications and often appeared to be unwilling to recognize or value their informal educational experiences as counsellors, mothers, political activists for example. The relationship was further complicated by the fact that I represented a different world in many respects. Much of my behaviour, language and accent reflect a middle class background and I have travelled a good deal having the opportunity to see and experience a variety of different cultural worlds. Most, though not all the women interviewed, had had little opportunity to travel as widely as I had done. They nearly all described themselves as coming from working class backgrounds. Their experiences of the world, their modes of communication and their cultural languages were in many ways, different to my own. It required a constant effort at the early stage of contact to find a way through these structural divisions and personal differences in order to discover and explore our common points of experience as women, and to develop levels of understanding and trust within which we could allow ourselves to admit some of our vulnerabilities and acknowledge differences as well as shared experiences.

A brief comment on the tendency in the research situation for the researcher to be labelled as an 'expert' is necessary. Firstly, it can be a way in which an individual or group can resist change and maintain the status quo if they have an investment in doing so. The researcher, by virtue of her accorded 'superior' status as 'expert' cannot easily belong to the group that has accorded her that status. In this sense she remains an outsider. Secondly, there are particular implications for the collaborative process. In this research model the researcher and researched

141

are trying to work towards a co-learner and non-hierarchical relationship (Maguire 1987). Labelling the researcher as 'expert' can be a way of resisting the collaborative process which because it may be unfamiliar may also be uncomfortable and threatening. Thirdly, it is important that the researcher is aware of the role(s) the researched place her in so she can recognize when she might be exploiting that role. There were several situations in which I felt particularly vulnerable. On such occasions it was convenient to slip into the 'expert/consultant' role and in so doing hide a sense of inadequacy or vulnerability behind an apparently competent front, thus reinforcing the 'expert' image.

Kirkup (1983) argues that one of the drawbacks of feminist participative research is that it places unrealistic expectations on the extent to which the researched can become involved in the research process:

> Even when problems are of a major concern to people (the researched) they have work and private lives which usually take priority, whereas research IS work for the researcher. (Kirkup 1983:24).

This reflects my experience. A consequence is that I found myself taking more responsibility for the research process than originally planned. In taking more responsibility I inevitably assumed more power and the 'expert' role became more difficult to counteract.

The role of the 'expert' under such circumstances is both powerful and lonely. It is of course only realistic for the researcher to expect to experience some degree of isolation in the research situation. However, this sense of loneliness was ironically exacerbated through the attempt to develop collaborative processes. While seeking to be a member of the group, you remain to a considerable degree, outside or on the margins. There is a constant tension in the role of participant i.e. involved with, and that of observer i.e. looking in from without.

No matter how much careful preparation the researcher might carry out before entering the field work situation, she will inevitably encounter elements of the unexpected and unknown. Reinharz writes:

> ...researchers working in natural settings become part of the political web of those settings, and the procedures they have prepared in advance in the sanctity of academia cannot neatly be operationalized. (Reinharz 1983:184).

142

Some of the difficulties encountered in seeking to develop feminist participative research illustrate Reinharz's point. What is clear is that the FPR process is complex. It demands a considerable degree of time, energy and commitment from both researcher and researched. The researcher requires a sound understanding of herself and the capacity to tolerate limitations in herself, others and in the overall research environment. It is precisely because FPR is such a complex process that the researcher requires well developed organisational skills along with qualities of perception, sensitive communication skills and flexibility. The reality is that these qualities are rarely available to the extent we might wish them to be! Thus the gap between the theory and practice of the FPR process is one that perhaps needs to be more readily acknowledged and more fully understood.

References

Bowles, G & Duelli Klein, R (Eds) (1983), *Theories of Women's Studies*, RKP, London

Brown, L D & Kaplan, R E (1981), 'Participative research in a factory', in Reason P & Rowan, J (Eds) (1981)

Cohen, J H & Uphoff, N T (1980), 'Participation's place in rural development: seeking clarity through specificity', in *World Development*, 8, 213-235

Coyner, S & Brooks, K (1986, April), 'Task force on feminist scholarship', Memo to NWSA membership, quoted in Maguire, P (1987)

Eldon, M (1981), 'Sharing the research work: participative research and its role demands', in Reason, P & Rowan, J (Eds) (1981), *op. cit.* 253-266

Ellis, P (1990), 'Participatory research methodology and process', in *Convergence* xxiii/4 23-34

Felizio, L S (1992), 'The task force on empowering women through health', *GADU Newspack* 15, Oxfam

Field, J (1991), 'Questions about research that make a difference', in *Convergence*, xxiv/3 71-77

Freire, P (1972), *Pedagogy of the Oppressed*, Penguin, UK

Graham, H (1993), *Hardship and Health in Women's Lives*, Harvester, London

Hall, B (1977), *Notes on the Development of the Concept of Participatory Research in an International Context*, International Council for Adult Education, Toronto

Hall, B (1981), 'Participatory research, popular knowledge and power: a personal reflection', in *Convergence*, 3 6-19

Hall, B (1992), 'Rich and Vibrant Colours: 25 Years of Adult Education', in *Convergence*, xxv/4 4-15

Heron, J (1981), 'Philosophical basis for a new paradigm', in Reason, P & Rowan, J (Eds), (1981)

Humphries, B (1994), *Understanding Social Research*, Whiting & Birch

Kirkup, G (1983), *Strategies for a feminist evaluation*, Paper presented at the British Educational Research Association's 9th Annual Conference, September

Maguire, P (1987), *Doing Participatory Research: a feminist approach*, Massachusetts University, USA

Mies, M (1983), 'Towards a methodology for feminist research', in Bowles G & Klein R (Eds) (1983) *op. cit.*

Mohanty, C T (1991), 'Under Western Eyes: Feminist Scholarship and Colonial Discourses', in Mohanty CT, Russo A & Torres L (Eds), *Third world women and the politics of Feminism*, Indiana University Press

Reinharz, S (1983), 'Experiential analysis: a contribution to feminist research', in Bowles G & Klein R (Eds) (1983) *op. cit.*

Shiva, V (1989), *Staying Alive: Women, Ecology and Development*, Zed Books, London

Stanley, L & Wise, S (1983), *Breaking Out: Feminist Consciousness and Feminist Research*, RKP, London

Welbourn, A (1992), 'Rapid rural appraisal, gender and health - alternative ways of listening to needs', in *IDS Bulletin*, 23/1 8-18

8 Doing service based research: Some lessons from the All-Wales Strategy

Mary Scally and Stephen Beyer

'It's been many things but it's never been boring' was a favourite saying within the research team towards the end of an evaluation of West Glamorgan's Staff Development Initiative (S.D.I.).[1] This might act as a summary of the experience of undertaking service based research as it can and, as we will argue, should involve researchers in a number of roles within the organisation, most of which are very demanding. This chapter outlines the experience of carrying out service evaluation in West Glamorgan and describes how research which started with the intention of working closely with senior managers soon met with obstacles that frustrated this intention. Circumstances forced a move to closer working relationships with other people having a significant stake in the initiative being evaluated, and involved the researchers negotiating a change in their remit, to take a more overtly developmental role within the service. The model of service development and evaluation which emerged from these new collaborations is described, which may provide one way for service users, carers and staff to be more actively involved in deciding what their service should be doing and in monitoring quality of provision.

When it was launched in 1983 the All-Wales Strategy for the Development of Services for Mentally Handicapped People (A.W.S.) was seen as a bold initiative calling for radical transformation of services for people with learning difficulties. The A.W.S. was based on an explicit set of values which required the provision of new services, and also implied a more positive view of people with learning difficulties and their contribution to society. The Welsh Office were seeking ways to promote these new ideas and to realign the attitudes of service providers, whose efforts in service design and face-to-face service delivery were recognised as being crucial to the success of the proposed changes. Funding was made available early in the ten year life of the Strategy for training to achieve this purpose. In response to this call for multi-disciplinary training, those charged with overseeing the implementation of the A.W.S. in West Glamorgan put forward proposals for an innovative model of staff development and received special Welsh Office funding to pilot this between 1986 and 1989. The Staff Development Initiative (S.D.I.) had the aim of integrating service and staff development, specific goals being the reorientation to A.W.S. principles of more than six hundred front-line staff, and the re-skilling of the work-force to implement the new patterns of services required. The S.D.I. sought to put all staff through a Foundation Course programme to raise their awareness of the problems facing people with learning difficulties and to change attitudes. These courses were to be facilitated by a group of 'Practitioner-Tutors' recruited on a part-time basis from within the service, and supported by a S.D.I. coordinator and a trainer. In a second phase service managers and Practitioner-Tutors were to come together with individual staff to plan a personal programme of in-service training to help develop the skills to match the changing nature of the services they worked within. In a third phase, Practitioner-Tutors were to be withdrawn and managers as a group were to take full responsibility for the continuing training of their staff, completing the integration of service and staff development.

Evaluation and its relationship to the S.D.I.

The implementation of the S.D.I. was overseen by a Staff Development Initiative Management Group which had as part of its brief obtaining an evaluation of the project. They produced a paper outlining the need for the evaluation which of course expressed the reasonable expectation that:

...the evaluation should be designed to show if the initiative had been effective and whenever possible to pinpoint the reasons for the successes and failures. (Management Group Minutes, Sept. 1984).

The S.D.I. Management Group felt it would be important to judge the effectiveness of the initiative by how well the concept of self-programmed learning had worked, and 'how people became involved in the S.D.I.'s programmes, what they learned, and how their attitudes and working relationships changed.' The group were clear that they expected any evaluation to play an important role in developing the programme (Management Group

147

Report, Sept. 1986).

The Mental Handicap in Wales-Applied Research Unit was approached to submit proposals for the evaluation and attract funding from outside sources to carry it out, but not until the initiative had been running for almost one year. This obviously represented a potential problem, as the assessment of change through training is logically dependent on measuring what the situation was like before training began. The majority of staff still had not gone through Foundation Courses however, and the interest in linking evaluation and decision making expressed by the S.D.I. Management Group left the researchers optimistic that a collaborative rather than a traditional 'hit and run' approach to evaluation could be achieved. Past experience had shown the researchers that the lessons learned during evaluation were not routinely translated into action to improve the service being evaluated. Patton (1982) had argued persuasively that much closer links were needed between decision makers and evaluators if results were to be used. The researchers decided to adopt an approach based on 'Collaborative Evaluation' (Patton, 1982) in which the primary stakeholders were directly involved in defining the evaluation questions relating to the S.D.I., and in ensuring the results produced were in a form they could use to decide on action to improve the service. Patton (1982, p71) has suggested that a collaborative group or task force should include people who 'represent the various groups and constituencies that have an interest and stake in the evaluation findings and their utilization'. At an early stage the S.D.I. Management Group seemed to be the natural choice as the primary collaborative group for the evaluation as it involved trainers and senior service managers who agreed expenditure on the S.D.I. budget and planned the S.D.I. programme.

Evaluability study

The researchers used a method known as 'Evaluability Assessment' (Wholey, 1977; Rutman, 1980) to formulate the required proposals. Wholey's model involved the researchers working through five stages:
1. Bounding the service to be analysed, determining what exactly constitutes the service and its objectives.
2. Collecting information on the service, through documents and interviewing managers and others to find out what they see as the service and its objectives.
3. Creating a model of the service that links what it does to its objectives.

4. Analysing whether the 'means' that constitute the service are likely to achieve 'the ends' they have as objectives, identifying methods required to obtain results, and what part of the service can be practically evaluated. This might include recommendations for additional work that may improve the evaluability of the service.
5. Feedback to the customers of the evaluation.

In carrying out this initial work it became clear that there were significant gaps in the design of the S.D.I., and the initiative was not being implemented as originally planned. The evaluability study clearly stated a fundamental problem:

> The S.D.I. may not be seen purely as a staff development exercise. One of the aims of the S.D.I. is to change the structure of services and the way they help people with a mental handicap to one which would be an expression of the All-Wales Strategy. There appears to be a lack of clarity regarding the process by which developments of individual staff are to be transformed into developments in service delivery as a whole.
> (Beyer, Evans & Todd, 1988, p15).

There were also signs that the arrangements for building on new attitudes among individual staff through individual staff development packages created by practitioner-tutors, managers and staff were breaking down, the number of post-Foundation Course meetings between all three decreasing towards the end of its first year of operation.

> ...The emphasis we have observed is on a 'bottom-up' approach to staff development, ensuring that as many staff as possible go through the Foundation Courses...keeping heads above water, and getting all direct care staff through Foundation Courses has been a major task for the relatively small number of staff it has been possible to recruit as tutors.
> (Beyer et al, 1988, p15).

The long-term goal of linking staff and service development through the primary involvement of managers as trainers also needed significant development before it could become a satisfactory target for evaluation, largely because of a perceived lack of service planning mechanisms at the individual service level.

...the goal of developing in managers a critical awareness of their service and a vision of where it should be going under the All-Wales Strategy, and then expanding the staff development role of managers is currently hampered by there being no plausible mechanism in the S.D.I. programme aimed at helping managers develop a direction for their units or teams. (Beyer et al, 1988 p25).

The evaluability study recommended that some evaluation time could usefully be dedicated to formative research in which those involved in the S.D.I. Management Group would spend time with researchers creating a clearer statement of the goals of the programme and specifying the mechanisms to be used to achieve them, particularly 'a more detailed statement of how staff development is seen as being linked to larger scale service development.' A proposal was submitted to the Joseph Rowntree Foundation for funding of the evaluation as it was anticipated that the collaborative nature of the research would enable these problems to be addressed at an early stage. The proposal was accepted and the evaluation began in 1987.

The loss of a collaborative forum

Problems began to multiply almost as soon as the evaluation got under way. The researchers had over-estimated the depth of commitment to a 'collaborative evaluation', and what this implied in terms of formal collaborative arrangements. They had also over-estimated the level of consensus between key actors on how serious the problems facing the S.D.I. were. The rhetoric had been that the S.D.I. was:

...a dynamic and open ended process which would be greatly assisted by the external evaluation since this would help ensure that the objectives of the S.D.I. are attained.
(S.D.I. Policy Issues Paper, January 1986)

and that the S.D.I. Management Group would provide the forum for that interplay. In reality, that view was subscribed to by only a few involved with the detailed design of the S.D.I., but only loosely understood by others who had more power and influence in the organisation, and many had little awareness of the practical implications of the evaluation process.

150

Between the submission of the proposal and start of the evaluation the S.D.I. Management Group was disbanded, the planning and management of the S.D.I. becoming largely the responsibility of the S.D.I. Coordinator. This decision was based on the view that waiting for Group agreement interfered with day to day operational decision making, and that the Group contributed little to strategic thinking on the S.D.I.. At this stage, the A.W.S. was in its fourth year, and West Glamorgan's budget for new services was growing to a point where it was becoming difficult to get new schemes started, and the grant allocations spent. The need to get new services running put pressure on the time of managers who were originally involved in the S.D.I. Management Group and it may well have been a relief to drop a commitment. In addition the situation put pressure on the S.D.I. Coordinator and his staff not to build-up large underspends through delays in courses or significant periods of reflection and redesign. However, with the disbanding of the S.D.I. Management Group the evaluation was deprived at a stroke of a component central to its methodology, leaving it with no immediate way of clarifying issues crucial to the success of the evaluation. In addition, ownership of the S.D.I. by those managing service delivery was weakened, increasingly allowing it to be seen as a staff training arm rather than as a fundamental component of a new philosophy of service provision.

New arrangements were eventually negotiated, the Principal Development Officer for services for people with learning difficulties, taking on the role of liaison person for the research. This arrangement had inherent weaknesses. The researchers needed the liaison officer to act not only in a traditional role as a sponsor for the research who is trusted by the setting, but as a principal actor, helping to clarify the programme being evaluated, and champion the use of research in key decision making fora. This may have been an unrealistic expectation, given that sponsors of evaluation in this position can be subject to a great many pressures. As Palumbo (1987, p21) has suggested, evaluation has multiple objectives:

...to help administrators understand and improve their programmes, another...to uncover the facts about a programme even if they are negative... Because evaluators may turn up information that can embarrass an administrator, it is difficult to find an aggressive, effective administrator who puts a high priority on evaluation. Administrators are not inclined to want their programme evaluated by an outside third party because they have little to gain and much to lose from them.

The ability of a research liaison person to promote cooperation with evaluation in the service and their ability to translate research into action may both be limited by the way decisions are taken within their organisation and their position within it. In the event, the liaison relationship became focussed on information sharing about general development within the service, negotiating access to key meetings, and in the later stages, on mechanisms for consultation and feedback.

Changes in the S.D.I.'s original design

The decision to do away with a representative body to manage the S.D.I. left the S.D.I. Coordinator as its primary decision maker. He recognised that the important work between managers, practitioner-tutors and staff to deliver individual skill development packages was not being delivered. He also recognised the threat the situation posed to the longer term objective of handing staff development responsibility to managers and to the main objective of integrated staff and service development. Still needing to ensure S.D.I. grant allocations were used, two strands of work were started to address these problems. First, a programme of pilot workshops was initiated with individual units whose staff had been through Foundation Courses, to identify what skills the staff would require given any changes in function the service was undergoing. If successful this was to take the place of self-programmed learning.

Second, a six month day release course was introduced for all first line managers of health, social services, education and the voluntary sector. In this course the managers were to be organised in three patch based teams and work through four exercises, which would:

a) identify their learning needs and ways to meet them;

b) improve their practice including job description, job analysis and action plan;

c) improve their service's practice through a similar process; and

d) improve their Community Support Team's performance.

It was hoped this would enable them to have a clearer vision of the way their own service should be changing to be in line with the A.W.S. and to help them take on responsibility for tailoring the skills of their staff to new patterns of working. In addition to these, the S.D.I. had started to respond to calls for team building workshops for newly formed services, and had instigated design work on workshops dealing with central themes such as individual programme planning, goal planning and basic counselling.

152

In retrospect, the loss of an effective S.D.I. Management Group led to a fragmented system of decision making in the project. While the S.D.I. Coordinator remained at the centre of that system, decisions about the content of various parts of the S.D.I. programme began to be transacted through a number of groups. Practitioner-tutors worked with the Training Officer on Foundation Courses, leading to changes in content from course to course. Members of the county's Development Team worked individually with services to look at the changes that were required and identify any associated staff training needs. While there was an initial structure to the managers course, the three Community Care Managers covering the county worked with the S.D.I. Coordinator to develop elements of it week by week, and facilitated the workshops themselves. In this complicated environment it became difficult to ensure decisions made within the context of a particular course were related to the broader objective of integrating staff and service development processes. From the evaluation's point of view, the researcher had to relate to at least four groups of people just to understand what the S.D.I. now consisted of, and for some elements the content was changing from week to week. This period could be characterised as flying down a hill desperately clinging to someone's coat tails, not being able to run fast enough to see where one is going, but not being able to let go for fear of losing them altogether.

Struggling to attain a meaningful evaluation

As the fluidity in the S.D.I. became apparent, the researchers adopted a two pronged approach out of necessity. First, the main component of the original S.D.I. model, the provision of twelve day Foundation Courses for front-line staff, had remained largely consistent over the first year of the evaluation, and the researchers were able to achieve the conditions needed to mount a summative evaluation to see whether the objectives set in original proposals were being fulfilled. The primary condition here was gaining the cooperation of practitioner-tutors to ensure participants completed pre-course measures that explored their attitudes to new service options for people with learning difficulties, and their knowledge of the A.W.S., what services were available and what other professionals did. The measures were completed post-course along with a set of measures relating to the delivery of the course (Scally and Beyer, 1991a). As one of the objectives had been to change the way staff carried out their work, it was important to look also at change in the workplace. The researchers brought

153

together a 'Focus Group' of participants from past and recent courses to illuminate the issues involved in applying the lessons learnt at work. This led to the creation of a questionnaire which was sent to all past participants to provide a more representative picture of outcomes in the workplace, and identify the factors which promoted positive change or acted as barriers to it.

Second, the researchers mounted a formative evaluation of the various new initiatives being launched. This involved gaining entry to the groups where the various strands of work were being planned, and participating in the workshops and courses to see what their objectives were, how they related to the original objectives of the S.D.I., and the extent to which the work addressed them. The researchers also carried out a series of interviews with senior managers from Health and Social Services, and others involved in the delivery of the S.D.I. and the services they were targeted at, looking at how they gauged the S.D.I's effectiveness. This strand of work was demanding organisationally because of the number of meetings needing to be covered, but it provided a wealth of information, in particular it showed that many of the factors affecting the S.D.I.'s success were located outside its direct control. Factors included the way planning of service delivery was carried out, and responsibility for strategic planning and development was separated from service delivery. The researchers became convinced that the S.D.I. could not succeed unless these factors were taken into account in a redesigned staff development system.

A change of role for the researchers

Eighteen months into the evaluation, with a summative evaluation of Foundation Courses and a great deal of formative work completed, the researchers reviewed their situation with the help of a group of advisors provided by the Joseph Rowntree Foundation. Although much had been learned about the changes taking place in the S.D.I., none of those outlined earlier had been fully successful. The managers course suffered from low attendance and, while some managers generated plans to develop their staff and service, others came out with idiosyncratic goals, unlikely to provide a clearer future for their staff. No process emerged to cater for the training needs they identified for themselves. While some of the unit-based workshops on identifying training needs for staff produced results, none ran their intended course and the idea was not taken up as a replacement for individualised identification of staff training need. The S.D.I. had by this stage effectively become a Foundation Course supplemented by a

154

series of unrelated short-courses and unit based initiatives.

The advisors agreed that the researchers were unlikely to achieve any more useful summative evaluation unless the S.D.I. was reviewed by the county, its objectives and its methods of achieving them re-established, and a more considered way of making decisions put in place. Without this the S.D.I. would be unlikely to achieve anything approximating to its original aims and the funders were unlikely to learn anything significant. It was felt that researchers now had enough information to change their role from one of hanging on to the coat tails of precipitant change, to one where they acted as consultants or facilitators to help bring about a more considered approach. Thomas (1982) has argued in favour of this approach by researchers:

> Social action research is instructive because it combines practice objectives, the formulation of an intervention and subsequent evaluation. .... the approach is valuable because it recognises the importance of analysis as an early effort in design and development. It is also useful because it tries to come to grips with how practice can contribute to the development of social policy. (Thomas, 1982; p20).

It is interesting to note in passing the impact that staff changes within the S.D.I. had on the role researchers took within the organisation. During the course of this evaluation the S.D.I. had four different Coordinators, there were two different Principal Development Officers, three different Chairpersons of Joint Policy Working Group, and significant turnover among Practitioner-Tutors, the Development Team and Community Care Managers. While there was some movement of these people between jobs, to a great extent the researchers ended up having the most comprehensive view of what had happened and why. This in itself put the researchers in a potentially powerful position with a responsibility to help people make informed decisions about the future of any programme. The researchers took a first step in this direction by writing a report, submitted to the county's Joint Policy Working Group, which highlighted the outcomes of the research so far. In this they stepped beyond their original brief, criticising service development planning and organisational structures within the county for the detrimental impacts they had had on the S.D.I.. The report highlighted the successes of the S.D.I. but concluded that while:

> ...there has been a great deal of innovative thinking displayed, and a lot of experience gained...some of the original concept of the S.D.I. as a coherent

155

and radical programme playing an integral part in service development has been lost...the difficulty is to gain a sense of how all this work has fitted together to form a coherent, planned, and most importantly, a managed approach to the development of services in the county.
(Beyer and Scally, 1988; p22).

The report discussed various approaches that could be adopted, but argued forcefully for a review of the S.D.I. involving senior managers from participating agencies which should result in:
a) a mechanism for managing the S.D.I. on which all agencies service users were represented;
b) a new plan for the S.D.I. which was part of a managed plan for service development drawing its authority from senior managers;
c) the plan only being changed after proper analysis;
d) new collaborative arrangements drawing on the researchers and their information as a resource.

The report was not well received by the officer group who prepared the agenda for the J.P.W.G.. It was described as unfairly negative, and not providing a fair assessment of the achievements of the initiative. The researchers were asked to resubmit the report in the light of the comments made. Initially, the researchers felt there was some truth in the observation:

If evaluations cannot be turned to the advantage of programme managers, then it is in their best interest to suppress or simply ignore them.
(Palumbo, 1987; p23).

More positively it validated the original intention of forming a long-term collaboration with senior managers, as the message would not then have seemed as stark or unexpected, arguments about balance having been handled as the research progressed, and people themselves having been involved in drawing detailed conclusions from the data. In the event, some minor re-wording was carried prior to re-submission, but the content remained largely the same. In spite of the initial reaction, the report acted as a catalyst, the J.P.W.G. later announcing that a multi-agency group with senior manager representation was to be set up to carry out a comprehensive review of the S.D.I. and re-design it. After nearly two years the evaluation had found the collaborative group it had hoped for at the beginning of the study.

This new role involved a range of new tasks for the researchers. When the 'S.D.I. Project Group' convened, the researchers were asked to be full members, and their report was used to set the agenda for the work of the group. They were asked to use their experience of what had happened so far in the S.D.I. to guide the group, and provide technical assistance in redesigning the project. In the initial phase of the group's work the researchers illustrated how service development planning was the key requisite to targeting training, by providing examples of how failures had impacted on the S.D.I. in the past. The researchers also provided information on Quality Circles and Quality Action Groups (Milner, Ash, and Ritchie, 1991) to support moves within the group to include a role for service users in any new system.

While being involved as observers in a variety of groups over the previous two years, the researchers had increasingly been struck by the lack of systematic involvement of either service users or front-line staff in reviewing service quality, or in service planning. The principles that had guided the original research design were that change was more likely to occur when those responsible for implementing change were involved in identifying shortcomings in their services, and achieved a sense of ownership of the solutions. If this was true for senior mangers in staff development, it was also true for front-line staff and the users of care services. As the focus of attention moved from staff development alone to staff development and service planning, it seemed important to involve a wider group of stakeholders in the evaluation of their services, in planning new directions for them, and in identifying the new competencies required by staff.

The new S.D.I. Project group recommended a joint system of service planning and staff development be set up, based at the level of the individual service e.g. house or patch based day service. The process was named 'Individual Service Development Planning' (Scally & Beyer, 1992a,b; Beyer and Scally, 1992a). The process would involve the service being given a set of design principles that set out what they were supposed to achieve. This would then be converted to a set of 'realistic service objectives'. A contract would then be formed between the service and the S.D.I. and Development Team for help to be provided in creating a plan for change over the course of a year. Individual plans would contain clear statements of outcomes for service users and harness training to achieve these, the success of the plan being monitored and reformulated at the end of the year. It was agreed that the process be piloted over a 6-month period so that the detail of each stage could be modelled, and that the whole exercise evaluated by the researchers. The researchers were involved in each stage of the design. By being directly involved in this way the researchers could ensure that the model was specified in enough detail and put into effect in a planned way so that its impact could be successfully measured.

The range of stakeholders involved broadened over the six month pilot period. A community based day service for people with multiple and severe disabilities was chosen as the pilot service, and the relevant Community Care Manager, service manager and a parent were brought into the project group. A stakeholder group involving two staff, the manager, a keyworker for a user, a parent and a user advocate[2] was established to follow the procedures developed. The stakeholder group were provided with a set of design principles drawn up by the S.D.I. Project Group, and then worked through a series of exercises, either taken from draft materials from the 'Quality in Action Project' (Milner, Ash & Ritchie, 1991) or designed by the researchers (Beyer and Scally, 1992b), to identify detailed outcomes the service should be producing for users. The stakeholder group then prioritised these and, for the purposes of the pilot, chose to work on giving people the opportunity to make choices, an opportunity often denied people with severe disabilities. The group looked at the large and small choices people could make during their week, and assessed the extent to which people were being supported in making these themselves. They then identified a series of opportunities to improve the situation, and who was responsible for bringing about change. These were incorporated into a draft annual plan.

Difficulty in communication between staff and users was identified as a common factor, the need for staff to understand the communication people had, and how to enhance it was an important area for staff development. This was seen as a key requisite to involve and empower service users. The service modelled contracting with the S.D.I. for a course designed around their needs. The manager and S.D.I. Coordinator worked together to identify some of the competencies this service's staff needed to have, and create a brief for a trainer. The S.D.I. Coordinator found the most appropriate trainer to do this work, the brief was revised with their expert knowledge, and a course was delivered.

Because of their direct involvement the work was planned to take account of the need for evaluation. The researchers mounted a summative evaluation of the work of the stakeholder group, and the impact the course had on staff, their performance in the workplace and on the reaction of service users. As they were party to the negotiations, the researchers were able to identify the changes the course was aiming to bring about in the service. They were then able to observe the aspects of communication between staff and users that were likely to change before the course, and to repeat the observations six weeks after the course. The evaluation showed small changes in a positive direction, with users being more responsive, and staff communication becoming clearer, more directive, and more often supported by physical help to ensure users were involved in tasks (Scally and Beyer, 1991b).

The results were still somewhat disappointing in the small scale of the change observed, and the overall evaluation of the pilot revealed an additional set of factors needing to be taken into account if training is to be translated in change in staff behaviour and produce real outcomes for users. In terms of the training itself, while directly targeted on the outcomes the service wanted to deliver for users, the changes required of staff were so large scale that they did not know where to start. The evaluation showed how important it was for managers to understand the content of staff training, and plan its implementation in a manageable way with appropriate supervision and support for staff. Personal supervision and positive monitoring by managers were important tools to aid this process. The broader evaluation involved interviews with members of the S.D.I. Project group, members of the stakeholder group, and all staff in the pilot service. The results were generally favourable towards the approach, although additional clarifications were required, particularly of the different responsibilities service managers and the stakeholder group model were to take, and the relationship between Individual Service Development Planning and county level strategic planning systems. After a year of additional work, the Individual Service Development Planning system is being introduced across the county in West Glamorgan in 1992/93, largely as it was conceived in the pilot.

Lessons from the evaluation of the S.D.I.

In retrospect, carrying out an evaluability study before embarking on a costly evaluation can be helpful in clarifying what the service is, what it is trying to do and whether it is likely to achieve it. For the exercise to be effective however, researchers have to have confidence in the results and push hard for any uncertainties it identifies to be resolved. The penalties for not doing this are clear. The researcher can be left trying to fulfil an evaluation contract that is basically untenable because the service is ill-defined, and undergoing constant change such that objectives, processes and outcomes cannot be properly tied together.

Being clear about the relationship between those commissioning evaluation and those carrying it out is also important. General statements and good intentions about collaboration between services and evaluations are not enough. The statements have to be backed up by clearly defined collaborative structures, and a commitment to a decision making timetable based on evaluation results. Researchers also need to be clear about who within the organisation wants a collaborative arrangement, and whether others also need to be in agreement for the arrangements to work. Without such agreements the contingencies of trying to spend money, political pressures to deliver within a tight timescale, and find answers to immediate crises, far outweighed those promoting the research enterprise and a considered approach to development based on research. This does not mean services have to be static over the course of an evaluation, but decision points timed to make best use of evaluation results are required if a form of disjointed incrementalism in service development is to be avoided. It is likely that when services are spending their own money on evaluation this accountability helps counter-balance other contingencies that may pressure them to take decisions that make the evaluation unworkable.

In the past the researchers have generally looked to carry out summative evaluation, and the original research proposal was framed in this way. The experience of carrying out formative research in the organisation to understand what is actually going on and why, even though forced upon the researchers by events, proved to be of great use in improving the S.D.I., and providing illuminating research material. The insight gained in this work enabled the researchers to move to a design and consultancy role within the organisation that helped a new model emerge, and also provided a much clearer basis for the summative evaluation of the outcomes of training. The fact that there were many staff changes placed an obligation on researchers to take on a more proactive role, as only a few others had an overview of the project history. In taking on this developmental role the availability of a group of outside advisors proved to be very useful, both in giving the researchers confidence, and providing advice on the approaches to take.

The experience of carrying out this evaluation has shown that mechanisms are available to enable those with a direct stake in the service to review its performance, and to plan for and implement positive change. If such participation is not inherent in the service culture, then evaluation will remain in

160

the hands of a few key people, usually over-committed senior managers. If collaboration between research and these senior people is effective, ownership of the change that results imply would hopefully be generated at a senior level within the service, and some coordinated approach to change ensue. While desirable, this would still leave the few people involved at this level with the considerable task of gaining ownership within the service they manage for the changes they want to make. If close involvement in evaluation can generate ownership and action among senior managers, then involvement in evaluation by service stakeholders can have the same effect. Increasingly therefore, evaluation needs to involve the primary stakeholders in the service; those who receive it and those who deliver it. Individual Service Development Planning and Quality Action groups offer ways of involving stakeholders, staff and users, to become involved in this work. In the future researchers should play a more active role in helping stakeholders understand their own services and the best ways to improve them. It will become increasingly difficult to justify service based evaluation which does not involve service users and those who act as daily mediators of service provision.

Notes

[1] This research was funded by the Joseph Rowntree Foundation and was completed between 1987 and 1990.

[2] An advocate was involved because of the level of communication difficulty those using the service experienced. In retrospect all agreed that direct involvement had not been pursued vigorously enough, and later in the life of the project attempts were made to involve directly those people who were able to express their views.

References

Beyer, S., Evans, G.& Todd, S. (1988), *Enhancing Evaluation : An Evaluability Assessment of a Staff Development Initiative.* Cardiff : MHWARU

Beyer, S. & Scally, M (1988), *The S.D.I. - A Positive Future.* Working Paper 5. Cardiff : MHWARU

Beyer, S. & Scally, M. (1992), *A Manual for Individual Service Development Planning System.* Cardiff : MHWARU

Milner, L., Ash, A. & Ritchie, P. (1991), *Quality in Action : A Resource Pack for Improving Services for People with Learning Difficulties.* Brighton : Pavilion Publishing.

Palumbo, D.J. (1987), *The Politics of Program Evaluation.* BeverleyHills: Sage.

Patton M.Q. (1982), *Practical Evaluation.* London : Sage.

Rutman, L. (1980), *Planning Useful Evaluations : Evaluability Assessments.* Beverley Hills : Sage.

Scally, M.& Beyer, S (1991a), *An Evaluation of West Glamorgan's Staff Development Initiative.* Cardiff : MHWARU.

Scally, M. & Beyer, S. (1991b), *An Evaluation of an Individual Service Development Planning System.* Cardiff : MHWARU.

Scally, M. & Beyer, S. (1992a),"Gear up for change", *Community Care,* 5th March, p16-17.

Scally, M. & Beyer, S. (1992b),"Design for living", *Community Care,* 12th March, p20-22.

Thomas, E.J. (1982), *Designing interventions for the helping professions.* Beverley Hills : Sage.

Wholey, J.S. (1977), *Evaluation and effective policy management.* Boston : Little Brown.

Welsh Office (1983), *The All-Wales Strategy for the Development of Services for Mentally Handicapped People.* Cardiff : Welsh Office

9 Anti-discriminatory practitioner social work research: Some basic problems and possible remedies

Bob Broad

This article outlines some of the problems to be addressed about anti-discriminatory issues and practitioner social work and suggests some possible remedies for them. After providing some examples of problems in relation to discrimination and social work practice and research it will then identify the processes whereby discriminatory and anti-discriminatory research can occur. These are located within tendency-to 'change' and 'no change' anti-discriminatory cycles. After identifying those cycles the agenda will move further forward to look at recent anti-discriminatory initiatives. Finally the article will present a suggested anti-discriminatory framework for conducting practitioner research. The use of a six stage 'gate-keeping mechanism' includes a practitioner research steering group. The first stages are choosing a research topic and groundwork and the last are conclusions and disseminating research findings. The author draws on some of his own experiences of being a researcher who is white, male and professional and seeking to be anti-discriminatory, to illustrate key points.

In this chapter the term practitioner social work research has a particular meaning beyond applied research by practitioners. It is used to describe supervised research by practitioners studying for a higher degree by dissertation, partly or wholly based on conducting a piece of research. Notwithstanding this focus, the anti-discriminatory principles raised in this article are, or should be, applicable to all forms of social research. The article does not set out to be a practical guide to undertaking anti-discriminatory practitioner research in social work although there is a need for one.

The term anti-discrimination rather than equal opportunities is deliberately used for a very important reason which needs explanation. It seems that in terms of its popular usage (rather than its intention perhaps) the term equal opportunities has come to mean all things to all people. If anything it has become a sort of umbrella term, mostly as written aims which cover a range of passive and active phenomena. In short it seems it has lost its punch. By contrast the term anti-discriminatory, meaning against discrimination (like anti-apartheid or anti-vivisectionist), indicates *actively working for change against all forms of discrimination and oppression.* It is its active ingredient and messages which are supported in the context of this chapter. Some years ago such a stance would possibly have been seen as unacceptable but there is now an increasing anti-discriminatory legislative and policy imperative in social work. This at last gives some authority and recognition to struggles about this issue in social work in the 1980s and 1990s. However in the first instance it is necessary to examine some of the problems that relate to anti-discriminatory issues in practitioner social work research.

Some problems that need addressing

The assumption throughout this article is that despite some progress in social legislation and practice the United Kingdom remains a racist and sexist society whose institutions systematically discriminate against a number of social groups whether in respect of unequal access to unemployment or other opportunities.[1] To varying extents social work practice will reflect those continued injustices. Therefore it is imperative that more recent initiatives, such as developments in practitioner research, do not perpetuate those injustices. Two of the key roles of practitioner research are to record and challenge those injustices where they occur, and second, where possible, to involve respondents and others in a participative way, rather than as passive respondents. Overall, practitioner research should be part of a process which is promoting social change. It should aim to be part of the solution and not part of the problem.

Some information from existing studies will illustrate why an anti-discriminatory approach to practitioner research, and indeed other social work research and practice, is necessary, first regarding the questions of staffing and monitoring. Eighty-six per cent of the social services workforce are women but just twelve per cent are directors according to a major report (HMSO, 1991: 1).

The report continues:

Thus whilst the delivery of services is seen as women's work, power and decision making remains firmly in the hands of men ... There is little

165

information on the employment of black and minority ethnic staff ... (HMSO, 1991: 1 & 9).

The position regarding the under employment of black staff and their over representation as clients in the criminal justice system (probation, police, prisons, youth justice) is also well documented (see, for example, NACRO, 1992). The pressing issue about black people being over represented in mental health institutions has also been recorded (see, for example, Cope, 1989).

Next here are some consequences of not having an anti-discriminatory approach to research, in a large urban probation service, with considerable training input in anti-racism for staff. A major inspection into probation court report writing concluded that the equal opportunity section of the report was "... the least reliable" (Inner London Probation Service, 1991: 12). But why? What were the issues that led to this unsatisfactory conclusion? As a member of that inspection team I know there was a gross under-representation of black officers in the group itself ("we simply can't get enough black officers into the group", said one senior manager), reflecting a wider under-representation of black probation officers in that service, particularly at senior management level (one at Assistant Chief grade as at 1991). In addition there was confusion at the *institutional* policy level about what did or should constitute anti-discriminatory report writing (could it, should it even exist?) as well as issues about methodology. I remember that there was a lack of commitment to move from gathering a random sample of reports for inspection towards a stratified random sample so that four groups, namely white male, white female, black male and black female were represented in the sample. Stratified random sampling, readers will recall, enables certain groups to be identified in order that they are not randomly under-represented in the total sample. In this case the 'necessary' data was not collected. Therefore without that data, the will, the institutional support or full consultation, the inspectors' final comment about the equal opportunities section of the inspection being "... the least reliable" is hardly surprising![2] To these examples about problems concerning anti-discrimination in research and practice must be added two observations recorded by Ahmed (1988). First that in relation to black communities there can be resistance to being the object of investigation and that there are often feelings of mistrust and exploitation about the use of data (Ahmed, 1988: 26). Second she records a tendency by researchers to follow subjects with which they are familiar. Hence she states:

166

There is a tendency that those working on research projects will exclude areas of experience that are most difficult, most controversial, and perhaps least familiar to them personally. (Ahmed, 1988: 19).

This comment goes some way perhaps to explaining why, when the majority of social work research managers, funders and policy makers are white, the experiences of black people, women and other discriminated against groups have been invisible and/or marginalised for so many years. However this tendency, militant or more likely benign, of researchers mainly to deal with the familiar is only one part of a cycle in which the choice of research subject is but one part.

Figure I is a diagrammatic representation of tendency to 'change' and 'no change' anti-discriminatory cycles in practitioner research and practice. Figure I (page 5) allows some of the problems already elucidated to be placed within a context and a system. It seeks to highlight two different ways in which the cycles of policy, practice, research and review can operate in respect of anti-discrimination. It deliberately acknowledges a link between research aims or intention, the process of undertaking the research and outcomes. In Figure I in the 'change' cycle the term 'equal access' is used to denote equal access to undertaking the practitioner research and/or social work practice. In the 'no-change' cycle, moving clockwise from the 'unequal access' position, it can be seen that if it is but one part of a wider organisational cycle of inequality then it is likely to reinforce rather than uncover structural inequalities and discriminatory practices. Marginalisation of views and perceptions will likely result if the power to define the questions remains in the unaccountable hands of the few.

Having outlined some of the problems and issues it is now necessary to look forward to what should or might be anti-discriminatory practitioner research in the future. This will be done first by looking at some hopeful signs and then going into more detail by providing an anti-discriminatory framework for practitioner research.

Some hopeful signs

It almost goes without saying that all activities are located within a broader legislative framework in which especially in the United Kingdom in respect of direct or indirect discrimination the Race Relations Act (1976) and the Sexual Discrimination Act (1975) and the Disabled Person (Services, Consultation and Representation) Act (1986) apply. It may also be the case in relation to black and

Figure I: 'Change' and 'no change' anti-discriminatory cycles in practitioner research and practice

(a) 'No change' cycle

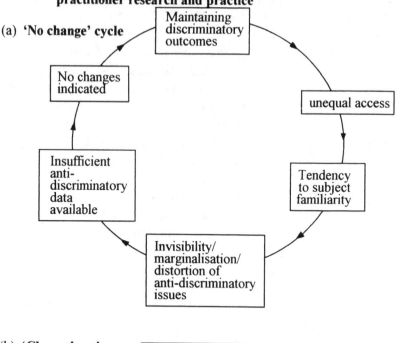

(b) 'Change' cycle

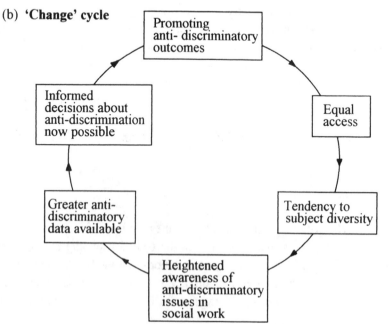

asian people that the United Kingdom's racist immigration policies will have an impact, in different ways dependent on the situation. Also for the first time ethnicity was recorded in the 1991 Census, as an information source. Additionally more recent legislation and a White Paper places greater legal responsibilities on social workers, for example, in the Children Act (1989) to 'give due consideration' to children of different culture, race, religion and language (SS61(3)(c) and 64(3)(c)); in respect of the 1991 Criminal Justice Act (S95) to monitor the ethnic origin of clients; and in the White Paper 'Caring for People' (HMSO 1989: 11) a recognition is given, albeit weakly, to the particular care needs and problems of 'people from different cultural backgrounds' in respect of the provision of services. Although these powers, duties and responsibilities do not go far enough, at least they are a beginning. In the future it is vital that anti-discriminatory responsibilities become statutory duties (not vague powers) and are regularly monitored and supported by regulations. Also the calls for service users to have more rights, including a right to receive anti-discriminatory services (see, for example, Broad and Denney, 1992) is a further hopeful sign.

In the social work training field itself the recognised qualification for social workers, the Diploma in Social Work, puts a requirement on students to 'recognise, understand, and confront forms of discrimination' in their work, as an anti-racism requirement for completing the course (CCETSW, 1989). In addition, there are other moves towards an overall anti-racist social work education (CCETSW, 1991, 1991a) and CCETSW post-qualifying anti-discriminatory requirements for social workers moving into practitioner research. Finally it is important to acknowledge that these messages are not only coming from government appointed bodies. There are, for example, Mullender and Ward's (1991) '5 practice principles' applicable to both practice and research. The fifth one which overrides all others in its application to social work practice and research states:

All our work must *challenge oppression* whether by reason of race, gender, sexual orientation, age, class, disability, or any other form of social differentiation upon which spurious notions of superiority and inferiority have been (and continue to be) built and kept in place by the exercise of power. (Mullender and Ward, 1991: 31, emphasis in original)

A detailed guide to 'equality issues' arising from the 1989 Children Act (Macdonald, 1991) provides a further indication of the range of issues that

169

practitioners and policy makers need to address to make anti-discriminatory work effective.

There are then a growing number of statements, statutory instruments at the 'ethical principles and requirements' levels in respect of various forms of anti-discrimination in terms of social work practice and research. Yet, as argued at the beginning, it is also at the practice and organisational level where much work still needs to be done to put these requirements into action in a systematic way. Hence a practical framework for conducting anti-discriminatory practitioner research is outlined. Figure II (page 8) reproduces that framework but first an important rider about its scope and application. The framework is produced as a suggestion, a starting point if you like, for readers fresh to this subject. With the enormous variety of research methods and designs available, and service users' abilities and interests the production of a blueprint for all situations would be impossible, as well as undesirable.

Figure II is a suggested anti-discriminatory framework for conducting practitioner research in comparison with social work practice.

Central to this framework is the concept of a monitoring system for the practitioner research. This idea is taken and adapted from anti-discriminatory Probation work, generally, and specifically from monitoring systems concerning the preparation of anti-discriminatory probation court reports. Where practitioner research differs is its insistence on including people independent of the researchers' employing organisation with direct experience of the subject being researched. Let us look at an example.

Example

Imagine that a practitioner researcher works within a social services department and sets up a monitoring steering group. The topic of the research is *comparing services offered and provided to black and white young females by the local social services office*. The steering group could include a group of young black and white female service users, or ex-users, relevant local black and white organisations, possibly parents and/or carers, social service representation at different levels including a balanced proportion of black and female staff, and the practitioner researcher. The gathering of a group, in itself, is not going to solve problems. Indeed it may complicate things. What is needed is a steering group with an interest and commitment, aided if required by being given necessary knowledge and skills. Using the 'higher research degree by dissertation' model of practitioner research here, the research supervisor would

170

Figure 11: A suggested anti-discriminatory framework for conducting practitioner research in comparison with social work practice

Social work stages	Monitoring	Practitioner research stages
CONTEXT Anti-discriminatory work consistent with individual commitment, organisational objectives and a team commitment		CONTEXT Anti-discriminatory work consistent with individual commitment monitored by gatekeeping panel
1 Social worker checks out equal opportunity issues which will affect the social work		1 CHOOSING A RESEARCH TOPIC Practitioner researcher locates a problem or question to be researched CONSULTATION/ NEGOTIATION
2 Social worker/ project worker is presented with a problem	Use of gatekeeping model	2 GROUNDWORK Practitioner researcher checks out and acts on anti-discriminatory issues which will affect the research CONSULTATION/ NEGOTIATION
3 Social worker is given/ collects facts which illuminate the nature and purpose of the problem		3 LITERATURE SEARCH Practitioner researcher searches the literature on the problem or question CONSULTATION/ NEGOTIATION
4 Social worker makes a plan of action within an anti-discriminatory framework		4 RESEARCH DESIGN Practitioner researcher designs a study CONSULTATION/ NEGOTIATION
5 Social worker carries out/ attempts to carry out action plan		5 DATA ANALYSIS/ COLLECTION Practitioner researcher collects material, analyses and collates it CONSULTATION/ NEGOTIATION
6 Social worker reviews work and may make new plans		6 CONCLUSIONS/ DISSEMINATION Practitioner researcher produces conclusions, disseminates information, and possibly makes recommendations

Note: This table is adapted from Dixon (1984: 4).

171

also need to be involved but not as part of the steering group. After sounding out and setting up the appropriate gate-keeping mechanism and establishing the terms of reference for the practitioner researcher it is then necessary to clarify the research topic's precise frame of reference, having established the general area of enquiry earlier.

Stage 1 - Choosing a research topic and its frame of reference

Practitioner researchers need to be aware and question others' definitions of 'the key issues' and 'the problems' to be investigated. In the example given a study based only on attitude questionnaires to 'clients' to 'examine clients' poor responses to services' in itself is biased and will be guaranteed to provide a one-sided view of the overall situation. It is likely, for example, that some people not responding to services are unwilling to accept the role that they have been ascribed by others. Other explanations are likely to include the service provider's function; their means and extent of service delivery; the existence and application of anti-discriminatory policies and training issues. With an anti-discriminatory perspective practitioner researchers need to both explicitly acknowledge and not deny the institutional shortcomings of British society, and not simply focus on impoverished individuals and families. As Lawrence (1984: 132) points out, ideas which fuel the accounts of some ethnic relations sociologists such as 'identity crisis', 'culture conflict' and 'inter-generational conflicts' run the risk of being constructed without reference to broader discriminatory policies, here concerning racism. It is crucial then for practitioner researchers to decide, in consultation with the steering group, by what criteria a particular issue merits investigation and by whom and for what purpose. Subtle and not so subtle assumptions permeate the history of discrimination and social work. These can relate to definitions of 'dysfunctional' black families or the labelling of black youths as being 'alienated because of their inability to become integrated within society'.

In one research study I conducted (Broad, 1991) it was found essential to fully record the differing perceptions about youth, especially black youth, as held by different professional groups (with all white representatives) meeting at inter-agency crime prevention meetings on housing estates following the Brixton disturbances of 1981 and 1985. The question of 'to what extent are the problems of youth but one part of wider problems for youth?' is important to ask. There are a vast range of social work issues which could become the focus for a practitioner research topic. Each of these has the potential to be interpreted and

172

misinterpreted - for example in relation to attitudes towards types of delivery at birth, the actions of health professionals, provisions towards pre-school children and types of mental health treatment and services offered by the criminal justice agencies. The choice of topic then, and its terms of reference are extremely important. What is also important is some basic groundwork by the practitioner researcher.

Stage 2 - Groundwork

Here groundwork means preparatory work by the practitioner researcher about the issues - a sort of personal 'sensitisation to the issues' education stage if the researcher is unfamiliar with the topic in hand. The purpose of this stage is to help towards subject diversification if the practitioner researcher is unfamiliar with the proposed research topic but does not want to use this as a reason not to study the subject. If the practitioner researcher is already familiar with the subject, either because of direct experience or through observation and reading, this stage will be less necessary but nevertheless desirable. There is a 'tendency towards subject familiarity' (Ahmed, 1988: 19) by researchers. If and when senior researchers are white-collar, middle-class and male (if this in itself is not a stereotype!), and this familiarity assumption holds true, then entire areas of life (the majority in fact) are excluded. For example I was unable to record in detail interactions at a women's group in probation (Broad, 1991) because it was a women's group and men were excluded. This was both a problem to me as a male white researcher wanting, for research purposes, to gain a fuller understanding of female offenders' issues but also for the female offenders themselves whose direct experiences of Probation group work remained unrecorded. This meant the research findings on that group were dependent on interviews and not, as hoped, on direct experience. Taking Ahmed's (1988) premise further, female white staff could find themselves excluded from black and white male experiences.

Whilst my ideological world is socialist-humanist, as a researcher walking through the door I am likely first to be seen as white, male and middle class (and conservative), and then as a researcher. This chapter argues that the relationship between ascribed and inherent characteristics impacts on social research. For example in participative research the issue of 'loyalty to whom?' usually arises, as one gets closer to respondents. Once when I was observing group interactions in an inner city employment programme for young offenders (Broad and Fletcher, 1983) I was bluntly told by one white working class employee "Oh yes, you're the f****** spy [for management] aren't you!'' Although I denied this accusation, and despite the fact that guarantees by me about anonymity were given and kept to, it was the business management group (white, middle class, male and female) that used its powers not to share my modest research findings with the workforce (working class, black and white, male). *I* needed and obtained direct access to the programme - *they* kept the findings to themselves. Also it could have been the case that the trust they placed in me derived, to some extent, from management's perceptions of what my class, gender, ethnic origin and age meant to them. On reflection I feared my research contribution only confirmed the 'no change' anti-discriminatory practice cycle outlined earlier in Figure 1 (here relating to class). However on the other hand the research indicated changes in work conditions and practices to improve access, attendance, productivity, and relationships, which were indicators for change in terms of role sets, gender and class.

Data that is selected, collected and then presented as facts does not derive from a neutral stance of scientific objectivity. It originates from pragmatism as well as from a value base, the social construction of ideas and propositions belonging to the practitioner researcher, and, if there is one, the funding body or supervisor(s). Unless a researcher is clear about the subtle nuances of racism exhibiting themselves in social work practice, in offices, in the culture of offices, written reports and the use of language, employment of staff and so on, then she/ he will have little chance of being able to observe and report on these experiences. Support structures and strategies may be necessary for researchers facing racism and sexism. Without an anti-discriminatory steering group or something similar, lies a huge potential for researchers, unintentionally perhaps, to follow and interpret topics familiar to them in the light of their upbringing, sexual orientation, class, gender based experiences and ethnic origin.

I am using this *groundwork* stage therefore to explore, before the research proper has begun, the relationship between three things: the selection of the research topic; the process of undertaking the research; and the possible effect of those two on the research findings. Another way of becoming aware of the issues, one central to all types of research, is that of the literature search.

Stage 3 - Literature search
The literature research stage is much shorter than the others but nevertheless important. By this stage a general topic should have been chosen, a frame of reference been established (though it may well be renegotiated later if it is a pilot study) and the groundwork largely completed. A literature search within an anti-

174

discriminatory framework needs to cross-reference the topic or topics being explored with any issues which may concern anti-discrimination. Based on the premise that only certain sets of data ever emerge in a printed form, it is especially important that a wide literature search is engaged in, involving information from smaller local groups, voluntary organisations, service users and campaigning groups. This is not to suggest these sources must replace the traditional library sources (where they do not already complement each other) but rather that both sets of information need to be sought, despite the extra time required! In a sense this is a second phase of the groundwork stage of sensitising the researcher, if necessary, to the topic(s) in hand. Again the use of the steering group is seen as necessary for this stage. Wherever possible the voices of service users in the literature, or on audio tape or video film, should be sought. The next major stage is the research design.

Stage 4 - Research design

In such a potentially vast area which includes both the overall design of the research and the choice of methods, a list of questions is produced rather than attempting to address all the issues which affect and/or impact on anti-discriminatory research and practice in detail. Prior to those questions, however, I want to comment first about classification in relation to research design, race and ethnic origin, and second about the complexities of participation and service users' involvement.

Classification of ethnic origin

It is vital to be consistent about the terms used and be clear about why one term rather than another is being adopted. The justification for what has become known as ethnic record keeping and monitoring is to establish who gets what services and delivered in what way. That data can then be put side by side with an organisation's anti-discriminatory policy statement and if it has one, impact statement. Unless the data is gathered, comparisons between different ethnic groups, special service requirements for ethnic and other groups, and the basis for comparing services against policy statements cannot be provided. The question of ethnic classification is complex and seems ever changing. In the criminal justice system in the United Kingdom the principle that there should be ethnic monitoring across all the agencies involved (probation, police, courts etc) was agreed by the mid to late 1980s. Yet in probation, for example, there has been considerable dispute about these classifications. Up until 1991, the Association of Black Probation Officers (Napo News, 1991) held what it described as a political definition of the term black (which includes both African and Asian people) to emphasise their common experience of, and their determination to, oppose the effects of racism. On the other hand Devine has argued that this political definition of black has been imposed upon certain groups, usually without their consent. As a result, according to Devine, Asian people are 'being asked to adopt an identity which is not natural to their being' (Devine, 1991: 249-250). Yet the categories under discussion above are political constructions. Devine's introduction of the additional category 'identity', here with assumptions about essentialism, is not directly relevant to arguments based on such constructs. To complicate things further, initially the Home Office (1987), in its survey of 'the ethnic origins of probation service staff' argued for the use of seven separate categories of ethnic origin.

It seems that the National Association of Probation Officers' support for ethnic monitoring was given so that "there would be a way of measuring the *impact* of anti-racist policies and action by the Probation Service and the Criminal Justice System" (NAPO, 1991a: 8). It did not require detailed ethnic classifications emanating from the Home Office to fulfil this aim. Eventually an agreement was reached between the five Probation interest groups (NAPO, 1992: 5) about ethnic monitoring. This consisted of some individualised information held on race monitoring ('black', 'white', 'other', 'refused' categories) as well as on ethnic monitoring, involving a choice of *52* categories of ethnic origin, held within 'the different areas' systems'. In this ethnic monitoring agreement it is stated that the Home Office's requirements for information would best be met by the collection of this individualised data but it is 'willing to accept aggregate data from probation areas' (NAPO, 1992: 5). The 52 categories are taken from the Office of Population and Censuses and Surveys (OPCS) categories as used in their censuses, so that, the argument goes, comparisons can be made. But categories such as Canada, USA, India, Hong Kong (taken from the 52) are not, cannot be, categories of ethnic origin but of nationality, and then not necessarily so in all cases! It seems as if this issue will run and run.

Then there is the thorny question of who should define somebody's ethnic origin? Wherever possible these should be defined by service users and if they do not wish to self define or include themselves in the research - so be it, providing they are given information about the purpose of the research and the consequences of not providing information. Service users could be offered a range of classifications, including 'other' (to be specified by the users) to encourage participation and self selection, albeit set within a framework of definitions. This appears to be the approach in Probation at the time of writing. With a practitioner research steering group including service users reflecting the diverse nature of British society as well as the particular interests of the research itself there should be less problems in this area.

Service users involvement

This broader issue about service user participation is a complex one which needs to be acknowledged. For full participation of steering group members and users who are new to the complexities of research design and methodology, there are major issues that need to be faced. First there is the important point that when conducting social research in a service agency (e.g. in social work or in health care) the agency's view of research, anti-discriminatory policies, and the ascribed role of service users will impact on the anti-discriminatory and participative research framework proposed here. It is likely that a hierarchical white male dominated service agency concerned with routinely putting and keeping service users in their place, as subordinate clients, will be the most antipathetic to the proposed research framework. The notion of power sharing with female black or disabled clients, as service users with a voice, may be considered as totally unacceptable in such agencies. There is also the more general point that there is likely to be staff resistance to the research's anti-discriminatory stance if staff and agency feel under seige, whether from service users, managers or service purchasers. On the other hand there are opportunities, for example arising from legislation such as the 1989 Children Act, to develop more consultative, accountable and open, and less defensive solitary social work styles. These developments should assist anti-discriminatory participative research. The earlier 'hopeful signs' section expanded on this point at some length. Perhaps some parts of the voluntary sector, and de-centralised services, can involve service users more than the centralised statutory sector in research.

I have been working on an action research programme with staff in a leaving care project for some time now. The action research was set up with many, but not all, of the principles and features raised in this article taken into account. In the fairly flexible voluntary organisation in which I work it has been possible to involve service users in the action research. Anonymous 'consumer satisfaction' questionnaires have been sent out by project staff to service users as well as to those commissioning the services (an increasingly important group in a mixed economy of care). Care leavers, as well as volunteers, are given a voice in the action research and they can decide, mostly, which information will be published about them. At this point in time their voice was 'given' to them by the professional power holders. I still intend to reach a point in the action research where service users' voices are heard, recorded, and published, as a right.

Yet service users' effective involvement in the research design and implementation, as steering group members, requires them to obtain skills and knowledge. Important knowledge can be acquired through greater service users participation in designing projects, user-friendly services and joining the committees of voluntary organisations. Additional research skills can be acquired from staff within the agency being researched. Also existing professional power holders can help non-professional service users by avoiding unnecessary technical jargon and/or explaining necessary technical terms and methods. It is acknowledged that all of these proposals require existing power holders, increasingly service purchasers and especially where the dominant group is white males, to give up some of their power. This needs to be done as a right in line with anti-discriminatory policies, and not as a favour in line with personalities.

The more general questions relating to research design centre around the areas of surveys, questionnaires, interviews and observations and I have produced here a number of key questions about these points.

Key questions concerning anti-discriminatory research design and methodology

- Is it likely that language will be an issue?

- Will interpreters be necessary, and will they be used?
- To rectify criticisms of state surveillance on black communities and in relation to survey research and reproducing Bowman's (1983) four points as questions:

-Will indigenous interviewers be used?

-Will the practitioner researcher be seeking assistance from indigenous community consultants or advisory groups?

- Will there be an initiating trade-off and exchange arrangements (for example, making payment to research subjects, making research available to research subjects, translated into a variety of Asian languages)?

- Will the research be targeted explicitly to the needs of black or other specific community groups and provide them with control of the research?

In relation to more general issues:

- How are issues of access for the disabled accommodated?

- How will the research for non-writers be accommodated? (They will need consideration and guidance in order to make their contribution to draft texts The taping of meetings and documents, as well as membership of the research's steering group will help non-writers' voices to be heard and acted on.)

- What research methods will be used to fully record children's experiences?

- Are there any religious festivals or other issues which will affect when and how the research is conducted?

- In respect of methods, how will the sampling frame be decided? (Recalling the earlier example given in the article.)

- What are the issues if participant observation is used or planned to be used as a method to collect data? (Recalling the earlier women's group example.)

- What are the possible gains and problems of involving service users in the research design and methodology? (Recalling the earlier discussion.)

- What structures need to be put in place to ensure the fullest possible response from those participating in the research?

Having raised a considerable number of questions which are necessary in respect of research design from an anti-discriminatory perspective, the final two stages have been combined, namely data analysis and report conclusions/

179

dissemination.

Stages 5 & 6 - The analysis, collection and dissemination of data

It is assumed that by these stages the data will be rich and comprehensive and needs to be collated and presented. Acknowledging the dual participative as well as anti-discriminatory aspects of the framework it is inevitable that the data collected will be first presented to the steering group. This is not simply for its consultation but for its guidance about what will be included and excluded and what ways will it be presented. It is of course possible to co-opt others on the group for these stages. However tempting, it is not possible to be prescriptive about such a vast area other than to highlight some key issues. The two selected are again language and accessibility. It has been argued throughout this article that this practitioner research report, study, or survey was intended to be sensitive to issues about equal access. Further that it set out to be participative and ultimately promote change, at the levels of policy and service deliveries. It is vital then, in terms of participatory aims, that the analysis of the data fully records the views of all those involved in the enterprise. It is also likely that there will be dissenting views about the data to be included. Wherever possible all views should be included in the main body of the report. However where this is not possible it is important that different views are represented and their authors acknowledged, again in the main body of the report. Ultimately it should be the practitioner researcher in collaboration with the steering group who have the authority to produce the report. If a consensus still cannot be reached about the contents of the final report despite the steering group's involvement at all earlier stages, then it may be that separate final reports, for example, 'agency' or 'steering group' final reports are produced.

It is almost inevitable that people will require a summary of any report that is produced with the main points being crystal clear. It really is of little help to busy people if a 60-page report, even one set within an anti-discriminatory framework is long-winded. Ultimately the task of and the challenge to practitioner researchers is to put across their messages in a clear fashion.

Recommendations to social work practitioners or managers should be spelt out clearly, within an anti-discriminatory framework. This should be done either by reference to existing equal opportunities policies within an organisation or 'self-standing' where such detailed policies and impact plans still do not exist. There is a further process, namely monitoring the implementation of the report's recommendations but this is not the task of practitioner researcher or steering group alone. Nevertheless, there should be one or two people within the steering group who represent the main organisation or organisations to whom the recommendations will apply and so there should be a full circle of research, policy, practice and review. Despite the more promising context for anti-discriminatory social work and research, the notion of an anti-discriminatory practitioner research framework may be seen as threatening to some. On the other hand it is only by promoting good practice, gaining support and presenting findings that issues concerning anti-discriminatory social work start to go on, or stay on, and move up the agenda.

I hope that this article has shown that, strategically, it is best to assume that the anti-discriminatory social research path will be strewn with debris. Some of it will be moveable, but some will not be and, therefore, structures, strength and conviction will be needed to travel along it. Yet in theory the anti-discriminatory research path is straightforward:

> If readers are serious about tackling discrimination, a systematic framework must be established in order to achieve this, both organisationally and at an individual level. Change will only occur if there is a genuine commitment to meeting the needs and aspirations of Black people as perceived by them.
> ... ARE YOU COMMITTED?
> ... WHAT DO YOU DO?   (Ahmad, 1990: 4)

Notes

[1] The evidence to support these assumptions is now voluminous and I do not intend to produce it here.

[2] It should also be noted that there was disagreement at local practitioner and team level about the issue of ethnic categorisation as well as the categories themselves which underlines the need for a systematic anti-discriminatory policy to have been produced.

References

Ahmad, A (1990), *Practice with Care*, London: Race Equality Unit, National Institute of Social Work, London: ACC Publications.

Ahmad, B (1988), *Race Equality in Social Services: Ways Forward*, London: Race Equality Unit, National Institute of Social Work.

Ahmad, B (1991), *Black Perspectives in Social Work*, Birmingham: Venture Press.

Ahmed, S (1988), 'Research and the Black Experience',in Stein, M (ed), *Research into Practice*, Proceedings of the Fourth Annual JUC/BASW Conference, Leeds University, September 1988, 17-32.

Bowman, P J (1983), `Significant Involvement and Functional Relevance: Challenges to Survey Research`, in *Social Work Research and Abstracts*, 19(4), Winter 1983.

Broad, B and Fletcher, C (1983), *Activity Groups in the Probation Service*, Cranfield: DSP Publications.

Broad, B (1991), *Punishment Under Pressure: The Probation Service in the Inner City*, London: Jessica Kingsley Publishers.

Broad, B (1991a), `The Use and Abuse of Power in Social Work Groups`, Paper produced for First European Groupwork Symposium, Imperial College, University of London, July 1991, *Report of the First European Groupwork Symposium*, London: Whiting and Birch.

Broad, B and Denney, D (1992),'Citizenship, Rights and the Probation Service: A question of empowering or oppressing Probation Service Users?', *Probation Journal*, 39(3), 160-164.

Caring for People: Community Care in the Next Decade and Beyond (1989), London: HMSO.

CCETSW (1989), *Requirements and Regulations for the DipSW* (Paper 30), CCETSW, London.

CCETSW (1991), *Anti Racism in Social Work Development*, Curriculum Development Project Steering Group: Leeds.

CCETSW (1991a), *One Small Step Towards Racial Justice*, London: Centre for contemporary cultural studies (1984), *The Empire Strikes Back. Race and Racism in 70s Britain*, London: Hutchinson.

Cope, R (1989), The compulsory detention of Afro-Caribbean patients under the Mental Health Act, *New Community*, 15(3): 343-56.

183

Devine, D (1991), Towards Real Communication: A Study of Confirmation Procedures in the West Midlands Probation Service, in CCETSW (1991) *ibid*, 250-58.

Dixon, N (1984), *Research and Planning in Barnados*, unpublished Barnados Paper, London: Barnados.

HMSO (1991), *Women in Social Work*, London: HMSO.

Home Office (1987), 'The Ethnic Origins of Probation Service Staff', *Statistical Bulletin* 24/88, London: Home Office.

Inner London Probation Service (1991), *Inspection of Social Inquiry Reports*, June 1991, London: ILPS.

Lawrence, E (1984), 'In the Abundance of Water the Fool is Thirsty', in Centre for Contemporary Cultural Studies, *Ibid*, 95-142.

Lawrence, E (1984a), 'Just Plain Common Sense, the "Roots" of Racism', in *Centre for Contemporary Cultural Studies*, 47-94.

Macdonald, S (1991), *All Equal Under the Act*, London: Race Equality Unit, National Institute of Social Work.

Mullender, A and WARD, D (1991), *Self Directed Action - Making Empowerment Work*, London: Whiting and Birch.

NACRO (1992), *Black People Working in the Criminal Justice System*, London: NACRO.

NAPO (1991), *Napo News*, The Bulletin of the National Association of Probation Officers, London: NAPO, (29).

NAPO (1991a), *Napo News*, The Bulletin of the National Association of Probation Officers, London: NAPO, (30).

NAPO (1992), *Napo News*, The Bulletin of the National Association of Probation Officers, London: NAPO, (43).

10 Empowerment and social research: Elements for an analytic framework

Beth Humphries

The notion of 'empowerment' has become a fashionable one, claimed as a fundamental value in a whole range of professions, across political divisions, and in social science research theory and practices. As a result in this country we hear of moves to empower clients, patients, pupils, consumers, respondents; the government pledges itself to empower citizens, passengers, parents; individuals are urged to empower themselves through for example the 'I will work' campaign, neighbourhood/car/thief watch, the (female and male) condom, saying 'No' to drugs and tobacco.

At the same time critiques of research methodologies from feminism, black sociology, participative paradigms, have increasingly addressed the power dimensions of the research process, and have been accompanied by attempts to share power with respondents by viewing them as 'co-researchers' or by emphasising commonalities between researcher and the subjects of research.

This chapter sets out to explore a number of dimensions of these developments, to examine more closely the concept of 'empowerment', and to identify ways in which it may be and is being incorporated into existing structures which subvert its emancipatory potential. In particular I am concerned to foreground the fact that 'empowerment' is claimed by so diverse constituencies as political groupings across the ideological spectrum, researchers representing a wide range of methodological positions and professionals of all value colours. This in itself is a cause for concern as I hope to show, and suggests that the notion is so ill defined as to accommodate any and all theoretical positions, and consequently to serve as a justification for oppressive practices.

The first task of this contribution then, is to explore contemporary understandings of 'power' and 'empowerment', and to suggest dimensions for a concept of empowerment which will take account of unequal social structures.

Such a concept should be grounded in values for research informed by ideals of social justice, and will serve as a measuring rod against which to evaluate claims to 'empowering' research.

Concepts of power and empowerment

What then might be some of the strands which should inform research committed to social justice? I want to draw on a number of theorists to bring together those dimensions which seem important in the development of a conceptual framework for empowering methodologies. I have been selective in choosing those aspects of theory which in my view are potentially useful, and have implicitly rejected others posited by the same theorists.

Any discussion of concepts of power must acknowledge the contribution of Michel Foucault (1978,1980), whose ideas, explicitly or implicitly pervade much of contemporary literature. His work has been interpreted and adapted particularly by feminists, and it is to Jana Sawicki especially to whom I turn for the results of her scrutiny of his work (Sawicki 1991). Foucault offers a theory of power which is potentially useful in constructing a framework for empowerment. His model has as basic elements

1. Power is exercised rather than possessed.

2. Power is not primarily repressive, but productive.

3. Power is analyzed as coming from the bottom up.

In this Foucault rejects the totalising assumptions in traditional revolutionary theory which claims that power is possessed; that power flows from a centralised source from top to bottom; and that power is primarily repressive in its exercise. He does not deny that this traditional model describes one form of power, but argues that it does not capture those forms of power that make centralised, repressive forms of power possible, namely the myriad of power relations at the microlevel of society (see Sawicki 1991 chapter 1 for a development of this). This interpretation of Foucault is important, since it allows for power which emanates from the state, class and the law, but at the same time makes way for the description of a network of power relations outside these centralised locations. According to Sawicki,

> ...by utilising an ascending analysis, Foucault shows how mechanisms of power at the microlevel of society have become part of dominant networks

of power relations. Disciplinary power was not invented by the dominant class and then extended down into the microlevel of society. It originated outside this class and was appropriated by it once it revealed its utility...
(p24)

In terms of empowerment we have presented to us dimensions of power which (i) allow that potentially, dominated groups may have access to power, (ii) emphasise its productive rather than negative potential and (iii) demand that resistance is carried out in local struggles against the many forms of power exercised at the everyday level of social relations.

This view of power can result in a clearer understanding of for example power relations inherent in the researcher-researched relationship, and reveals not a simple hierarchical loading based on socially ascribed characteristics, but complex multifaceted power relations which have both structural dominance and structural subordination in play *on both sides*. Bhavnani (1991) illustrates this in her research as a black woman researcher interviewing black and white 16-year-old working class people, "...social research can avoid being synonymous with social stereotyping and instead, become important in the construction of different sets of discursive realities about particular groups - those realities being both resonant with and reflective of, the material realities" (Bhavnani 1991, p144). Here Bhavnani identifies both the contradictions inherent in one's location within various structures, and the ongoing importance of the material realities of people's lives. I shall return later to the contradictions, but here focus on 'the material realities' since it is the absence of this dimension for which discourse theory (and postmodernism generally) has been criticised. And it is such an element which is necessary to any conceptual framework grounded in social justice.

Kate Soper, in an attempt to make sense of the attack by postmodernism on socialism as a 'totalising credo', sees a constructive potential in the impact of 'difference politics' (Soper 1991). She suggests that new forms of communication are opening up across the 'realist' versus 'postmodernist' divide. At the same time, she warns of postmodernism's contrary as well as progressive potential for change:

There is a risk... that under cover of the very respectable request that we acknowledge difference, we justify as forms of self-expression what we ought to denounce as modes of greed, narcissism and egoism which are all too little considerate of the basic needs of others; or that in challenging the political collective as a false form of humanism we grant legitimacy to what are actually very disquieting forms of tribalism; or to be even more polemical, that in allowing an analysis of all the more ugly - racist, nationalist, sexist - tropes of our times as reactive reassertions of 'difference' induced by human discourse itself, we give the green light to a discursive neo-fascism. In other words, to grant all the rope to 'discourse' and none of it to 'reality', is to put the noose round those cardinal values of equality and democracy in whose name all serious struggle against oppression must be conducted... (p108)

I have included this long quote from Soper because it is an eloquent expression of the nub of my concern. An empowering research methodology cannot be constructed in a theoretical cul-de-sac or a values vacuum, and thus become a hostage to fortune. It must be grounded in the (unfashionable) struggle against structured oppression.

Sivanandan, in his attack on the identity politics of the new social movements, reminds us that all the radical social and cultural changes we are experiencing now, derive from the economic - still (Sivanandan 1990). He argues that the battle is not about the 'subject' or 'culture', but still about the ownership and control of the means of production and the exploitation of workers. However the new productive forces have succeeded in dispersing ''all the bits and pieces of the working class'' (p8) - the peripheral workers, home workers, ad hoc workers, casual, temporary, part-time workers. For our purposes here in constructing a framework for empowering methodologies, Sivanandan offers perhaps the most fundamental ingredient:

The touchstone of any issue-based or identity-based politics has to be the lowest common denominators in our society. A women's movement that does not derive its politics from the needs, freedoms, rights of the most disadvantaged among them is by that very token reformist and elitist.
Conversely, a politics that is based on women qua women is inward-looking and nationalist, and above all, failing of its own experience. So too the blacks or gays or whoever. So too are the Green and Peace movements Eurocentric and elitist that do not derive their politics from the most ecologically devastated and war ravaged parts of the world. Class cannot just be a matter for identity, it has to be the focus of commitment. (p19)

Here Sivanandan is not arguing against issue-based campaigns or research, but is appealing for the opening up of specific, particularistic oppressions to be informed by other oppressions, and committed to the needs of the poorest, thus avoiding what he calls a 'new sectarianism' (p10).

Mohanty, from a feminist perspective, takes this analysis further by calling for urgency in understanding the complex *relationality* that shapes our social and political lives, and by suggesting relations of power that are not reducible to binary oppositions or oppressor/oppressed relations:

> I want to suggest that it is possible to retain the idea of multiple, fluid structures of domination which intersect to locate women differently at particular historical conjunctures, while at the s ame time insisting on the dynamic oppositional agency of individuals and collectives and their engagement in 'daily life'. (Mohanty 1991,p13)

Mohanty draws on the work of Dorothy Smith who insists that not only can different oppressions 'inform' one another, but that they are interconnected through what she calls 'relations of ruling':

> a complex of organized practices, including government, law, business and financial management, professional organization and educational institutions as well as discourses in texts which interpenetrate the multiple sites of power. (Smith 1987,p3).

Here Smith identifies knowledge, social institutions and individual consciousness and experience, and emphasises in Mohanty's words the *process or form* of ruling, not the frozen embodiment of it' (Mohanty 1991, p14) as a focus for analysis.

Mohanty calls for the contours of the world we live in to be defined in relational terms, traversed with intersecting lines of repression and resistance; a world understood in terms of destructive divisions of gender, colour, class, sexuality and nation, but one also of powerful histories of resistance in daily life and as organised liberation movements. Following Foucault, she rejects a binary division of power which represents power relations as

> ...structured in terms of a unilateral and undifferentiated source of power and a cumulative reaction to power - which in turn is possessed by certain groups of people. The major problem of such a definition of power is that it locks all revolutionary struggles into binary structures - possessing power versus being powerless. (Mohanty 1991a,p71).

Such simplistic formulations in her view are historically reductive, and are ineffectual in designing strategies to combat oppressions. She argues for a mode of inquiry which is based in autonomous, geographically, historically, culturally grounded feminist concerns and strategies. In adopting such a position, western feminists (and others) might avoid a research focus which searches for examples of 'powerless' third world women (or whomever) to prove the point that women as a group are powerless. Instead we will seek to uncover the material and ideological specificities that constitute a particular group of women as 'powerless' in a particular context. Mohanty's words have echoes of Bhavnani's as quoted earlier,

> [Feminist] struggles are waged on at least two simultaneous, interconnected levels: an ideological, discursive level which addresses questions of representation..., and a material, experiential, daily-life level which focuses on the micro-politics of work, home, family, sexuality, etc.
> (Mohanty 1991,p21)

Elsewhere in her article Mohanty underlines Sivanandan's concern to ground these understandings especially in the daily life struggle for survival of poor people.

This brings us to a point where some of these themes can be brought together to trace a framework for empowering research methodologies. As I see it, the important strands identified here include,

(i) a view of power which on the one hand involves multiple, fluid structures of ruling rather than fixed and binary opposites;

(ii) and which on the other hand is exercised rather than possessed, and is therefore potentially available to dominated groups, who also have histories of oppositional agency;

(iii) multifaceted power relations experienced as contradictions in structural dominance and structural subordination on both sides;

(iv) a fundamental economic basis of oppression which demands an analysis at levels of both discursive and material realities;

(v) the historical, geographical, cultural specificity of oppression and issues of concern;

190

(vi) the grounding of any analysis in the struggle for survival of the most disadvantaged and the poorest, not in the privileging of a particular group as the norm or referent.

I propose to use this framework both to critique research which claims to be 'empowering' but in my view is not, and to illustrate the empowering impact of research which clings to and is framed around these parameters. The discussion focuses in turn on three themes which I see as problematic in some research approaches. I have called these *accommodation, accumulation and appropriation*. They are not of course entirely separate but in practice interrelate to produce and reproduce oppressive structures. They are taken separately as a way of assisting the analysis.

Accommodation

One of the most insidious processes in professional and research practice related to empowerment, is the accommodation of challenging and 'dangerous' (dangerous that is, to the status quo) ideas to ensure they conform to already established vocabularies and beliefs. Research studies which purport to have empowerment as a goal often result in an accommodation of commonly held beliefs, and the beneficiaries are more likely to be the research professionals than the research subjects.

As a result of these processes what we have, in Edward Said's words, is *reconstruction* and *repetition*. In a different context he describes

...a set of structures inherited from the past, secularised, redisposed, and re-formed...In the form of new texts and ideas, (the East) was accommodated to these structures... (Said 1978, p122).

An example of this is found in the October 1992 issue of *Research on Social Work Practice*. It contains a report of research which illustrates the points I am trying to make. The article describes a study undertaken

to determine whether or not African-Americans themselves experience a skin color bias directed against fellow African-Americans (Hall 1992, p479).

The conclusion of the research was that a group of African-American students evaluated darker skin colour in a negative manner and viewed lighter skin tones as more desirable. Hall suggests that this has implications for social work because of the psychological impact on self-esteem and self-concept, and the need for social workers to be made aware of such bias in their own practice.

My concerns about the potential for accommodation to established views and prejudices are several:

(i) Its theoretical assumptions. Hall does not acknowledge the deep divisions and inequalities in American society (see for example Edsall 1984) as a basis for his study. His explanation for colour prejudice is:

> Because the majority of Americans have been of European descent, light skin color became the ideal.   (Hall 1992, p480).

The irrationally of this is lost on Hall, since how does one explain societies where white skin is seen as desirable where the *minority* are white?

In his general discussion Hall conflates on the one hand any notion of unequal chances in education, work and positions of power, with on the other prejudices amongst people of similar racial origins. These become indistinguishable in the text. There is no association with a history of dominant ideologies and denial of human rights, of colonialism and exploitation. There is no understanding of the politics of black communities. Given the conditions of exploitation, it would be remarkable if such divisions did not exist amongst African-Americans.

But the crucial point here is, by not setting the events being described in a larger historical, economic and political context Hall uses concepts as parameters which make such research far from empowering and open up the way for victim-blaming ideologies.

(ii) Its methodology. We are told that the sample consisted of 83 (33 men and 50 women) African-American first-year college students attending a historically black college in South Georgia. The respondents were asked to rate their skin colour on a five point scale from 'lightest' to 'darkest'. They were also requested to complete a number of sentences which would 'express your preference about Black Americans...'. The choice of responses was again from a five point scale from 'lightest' to 'darkest.' Below are some examples of the incomplete sentences:

192

- Pretty skin is _____
-The skin color of smart Blacks is _____
-The skin color of Blacks who are kind is _____
-The skin color of my family should be _____
-The skin color of Blacks who are dumb is _____

The author tells us:

> Those rating themselves as lightest or lighter composed the lighter group (n=57), whereas those providing self-ratings of dark or darkest composed the darker group (n=26). *Those rating themselves as medium were not analyzed in this study..* (Hall 1992, p483, emphasis mine).

Scores were allocated to the answers, with higher scores reflective of a greater valuing of lighter skin and a devaluing of darker skin. Lower scores reflected a greater valuing of darker skin and a devaluing of lighter skin.

An immediate flaw in all of this is the absence of any information on those who chose the 'medium' category, or indeed any explanation regarding the omission. Since the 57 lighter and the 26 darker add up to the 83 we were told were in the sample, the original number taking part in the sample must have been higher than 83 if some were excluded from the analysis. The information we are given therefore becomes meaningless, indeed suspect, and we must ask questions as to why some information is withheld and why the analysis is not complete.

A further problem is the appropriateness of such a methodology for this kind of research. Hakim (1987) has drawn attention to the limitations of such surveys when the information sought extends to social contexts and interactions within groups and neighbourhoods. In other words, the data required is much more complex than can be captured by a one-dimensional instrument offering a narrow, prescribed range of responses, and problems of reliability, quality and hence interpretation arise.

Despite these concerns, Hall was able to make a generalised claim that his research showed

> ..light-skinned African-American college students value lighter skin tones more highly, relative to dark-skinned students... (p484).

193

(iii) Its implications for practice. The conclusions of the study are that more awareness on the part of social workers is needed to the impact of all this on self-esteem and self-concept:

> ...teen pregnancy, generational welfare and drug abuse may indeed be symptoms of a more deeply rooted inability to resolve skin color issues in a color-biased society...

It was also suggested that:

> ..light-skinned African-American human service professionals may be more highly sought after as therapists by Black clients.. (p484).

Thus, research which purported to improve services to black communities by increasing understandings of the nature of oppression, concludes with a individualistic and pathologising view of the research subjects. They can now legitimately be viewed as prejudiced against each other and therefore to blame for - or at least not doing much to alleviate - their own ills. Counselling to resolve the resulting problems becomes part of professional practice, and Hall suggests social work educators

> ..may begin by adding skin color to the curriculum. (p484).

It is the professionals who gain most in all this, by a call for a development of their repertoire of professional skills to include an 'understanding' of conflict within black communities. The structures of a racist society are left intact and the way is opened up for an accommodation of potentially disruptive knowledge to established beliefs and practices.

In this research there is no theory of power or historical, geographical or cultural contextualising of the issues; there is no acknowledgement of the contradictions inherent in the experiences and politics of black communities; no hint of oppositional agency; no understanding of racist discourses or material realities; and no analysis grounded in anything other than the author's beliefs and assumptions.

A different story: Black women and violence

Contrast Hall's study with Amina Mama's (1989) research on British statutory and voluntary sector responses to violence against black women in the home. This was the first comprehensive study in Britain to look specifically at the experience of domestic violence of women of African, Asian and Caribbean backgrounds.

The similarity with Hall's study is that the starting point was the oppression of black people within their own communities. This might have set the scene for a similar treatment which would offer a narrow description of the horrors of violence perpetrated on black women by (largely) black men, and which would have led to the conclusion that (a) black women are perpetual victims, (b) black men are inherently more violent than white men, and (c) the caring services need to learn more about this phenomenon and develop appropriate skills to counsel and console.

In fact Mama avoids all of these pitfalls. She adopts a theoretical framework which starts with the premise and illustrates that violence against women is a worldwide phenomenon. Men who abuse are from a range of social classes, cultural and religious backgrounds and include both white and black men. The expression of violence is culturally and geographically specific:

...the privatised and hidden character of 'family life' operates to mask the everyday atrocities referred to as domestic violence in advanced capitalist contexts like Britain, and that violence is all the more hidden in black communities because of racism...

in many countries of Africa, Asia and the Americas, domestic violence has to be understood in the context of the widespread structural violence produced by the extreme class, gender and racial inequalities that characterise life. Poverty, social disorganisation and political repression are just some of the factors... (Mama 1989, p299)

Furthermore, the choice of focus for the research was not, as in that of Hall, the dynamics and details of conflict within the black community, but the help or otherwise received by women in seeking to *flee* violence. This shifts the spotlight on to the processes of state bureaucracies operating in a racist society.

Mama argues that any analysis must incorporate both the history of black people and current international relations. She identifies both discursive (eg. racist immigration laws, popular culture and political discourses) and material levels (eg. black and working class women's unequal situation in the labour market, problems obtaining decent housing and protection, the commodization of social relationships), and she grounds her analysis in, and derives her politics from what Sivanandan refers to as '...the needs, freedoms, rights of the most

195

disadvantaged...' (Sivanandan, 1990, p9). Within this broad context she is able to examine black women's experience of violence without pathologising black communities.

Mama's methodology reflects a desire to reduce inequality in the research process, and the issue of power between the researchers and the research subjects is confronted directly. Strategies for achieving this include ethnic matching of the researchers with the subject group. Black women's accounts of their experience were the major source of information:

> it was assumed that the people who knew most about what happens to black women who experience domestic violence were those who had had that experience. (p29).

As a result of this, the researchers were able to identify women's oppositional agency everywhere, whether through formal organisation on a global scale, or through individual resistance specific to this study.

The views of relevant professionals were also taken to be credible accounts of what occurs from the perspective of their institutional roles, *but their accounts were not taken to be more credible than the accounts of those they 'process'.*

The theoretical understandings and the methodology are seen to be interdependent in Mama's research,

> ...care was taken to use an approach which, throughout the research process, integrated a range of methods with the analysis and theorising...there is no method without an implicit theory, and no theory that does not have methodological implications. (p28).

Moreover, and most importantly, the analysis was conducted in the light of people's collective histories and cultures. This included for example British history and culture, and the organisational culture of large local state bureaucracies; the history of Britain's relations with black people was also taken into consideration - colonial conquests, enslavement and economic exploitation; the particular history of relations between black women and British institutions was a central pivot; it was also assumed that present day international relations affect the treatment of particular national groups and those who apparently look like them (eg. changes in the treatment of Nigerians and Ghanaians by immigration authorities filter across and influence the behaviour of all other state agencies - the police, social services, housing, etc.).

196

Mama's conclusions illustrate the unequal treatment and oppression of black women by state and voluntary organisations, compounded by the stigma that attaches to abused and single-parent women. Actions which she recommends to ameliorate the situation faced by black women subjected to violence, assume primarily that segregation and exclusion from services is a result of political processes, that politics is about both regulation *and* contestation, that power is the potential to create history, and that therefore the means to 'empowerment' is through *political processes and political struggle* (Bhavnani 1991).

Mama's study identifies the need for changes in the law relating both to domestic violence and immigration; it calls for more informed responses by state agencies, especially the urgent need for safe and decent housing for black people; it identifies the need for police responses to be appropriate, effective and efficient enforcement of the law; and it wants educational and campaigning work and organising to take place within black communities where women-abuse is often hidden and excused on completely erroneous grounds. It identifies the need for black mental health services to provide supportive counselling for black women subjected to violence.

All of these strategies place the need for change squarely on social structures and on communities, and avoid heaping blame on 'victims'. They also place counselling and individual support appropriately amongst a range of wider actions - not as the sole means for 'coming to terms with' and 'adjusting to' their experiences. Throughout the study, from the setting of the conceptual framework to the last recommendations, Mama refuses an accommodation of pervasive prejudices about black women and men.

Accumulation

I have borrowed the concept of 'accumulation' from Edward Said (1978), in order to facilitate the examination of another dimension of disempowering research studies. Said demonstrated how modern Orientalism tends towards a systematic accumulation of human beings and territories through colonialism and imperialism. It organised itself as the acquisition of Oriental material and its regulated dissemination as a form of specialised knowledge. The result is a mass of artefacts and 'data' representing the East which includes,

a vast depot of objects of all kinds, of drawings, of original books, maps, accounts of voyages... (Sacy, as quoted by Said, p165).

197

In other words according to Said, Orientalism domesticated knowledge to the West,

> filtering it through regulatory codes, classifications, specimen cases, periodical reviews, dictionaries, grammars, commentaries, editions, translations... a sort of imaginary museum without walls (p166).

Said describes this process as not so much a way of receiving new information as it is a way of controlling what seems to be a threat to some established view of things (p59).

I want to use this notion to suggest that an outcome of some research efforts is an *accumulation* of information about the lives of oppressed groups, communicated through a specific language which in turn results in surveillance and regulation rather than 'empowerment'.

Frank Mort's investigation of how ideas of health and disease are linked to moral and immoral notions of sex, is reported in *Dangerous Sexualities* (Mort 1987). Taking reporting on AIDS as a starting point, and regarding it as a contemporary moment in a much longer history, he examines official and historical documents from the nineteenth and early twentieth century. He offers a detailed account of the relation between systems of medical knowledge and power, and analyses the way medical and other discourses have produced a distinct regime of sex, targeting sensitive or dangerous groups and generating forms of resistance. He in conclusion returns to the narrative of AIDS, working, in his words 'between the contemporary and the sexual scripts handed down to us' (p211).

For the purposes of this chapter I want to extract from his work the possibilities for empowering research in exposing the moral overtones inherent in much of accumulated 'facts', which are rather *representations* of the lives of the poor and the oppressed. At the same time we can also draw from Mort's work those *resistances* to the official narrative, those oppositional political forces which engage in the struggle for meaning and for material change.

Mort's examination of official public health records, state administration and government documents from the 1830's onwards reveals two central themes: *a link between poverty and immorality (particularly of the urban poor) and disease; and the discovery that disease spread from the dissolute to the sober and industrious.* These ideas were formulated within the languages of social medicine, and it was this professional discourse which provided pioneers in the field with the legitimacy to scrutinise the physical and moral health of the

198

labouring classes. Research into the material conditions and habits of life of the poor accumulated information which confirmed the equation between poverty, (sexual) immorality and disease. As Mort puts it,

Gothic images of horror, Old Testament style narratives of pestilence and pollution, dramatized through personal encounters and heavily resonating metaphors - all this was commonplace. The language of moral frisson, combined with the methodology of scientific inquiry, constructed sexuality at the heart of its concerns   (Mort 1989, p22).

These themes according to Mort were to the fore in all the official inquiries, but were particularly dominant in the blue books on sanitary reform. Descriptions of the wretchedness of working-class environments led to classification of specific immoral acts. Mort's account contains numerous quotes from research documents which consistently offer 'facts' which are laden with moral overtones.

Filthy habits of life were never separated from the moral filthiness for which they were the type and the representative   (p39).

The important aspect of all this is that these definitions were incorporated into a variety of 'official' knowledge which led to programmes of state intervention. For example the contagious diseases legislation concerned itself with the sexual and moral habits of two particular groups within the urban poor - female prostitutes and the lower ranks of the armed forces. Yet, although protocols of official inquiry were employed, this 'official' knowledge did not transparently render a true picture of reality - its accumulation was filtered through medico-moral lenses which actively constructed and objectified 'the sexual'.

In Mort's view this accumulation and representation of the life of the poor reveals specific social practices - the active construction of a reality which would lead to the regulation of sexuality, and the construction of class power and knowledge. The collection of information which would ostensibly lead to cure for disease was edited, resituated, rescheduled and presented in ways which defined and contained the sexuality of particular groups. It simultaneously distanced the culture and the habits of the reformers and professionals.

In this work Mort employs a research methodology which sets contemporary debates about AIDS in an historical, political and economic context, and which demonstrates how apparently objective 'facts' are overladen by moral discourses which have the purpose of controlling the sexual behaviour of certain social groups. Against the historical background provided by Mort, it becomes clear that the AIDS narrative in the late twentieth century occupies a distinctive place in the ideological repertoire of the moral right, by allowing a space to push for

> a new order of moral absolutes, pointing up links between moral and social and political instabilities. (Mort 1987, p214).

The 'logic' which emerged from the array of symptoms, pointed to a connection between the lifestyles of gay men and the spread of AIDS, and some of the early research focused on collecting 'facts' about the sexual behaviour of gay men (indeed the researchers themselves were often gay men, because of their likely access to gay men's lifestyles). Mort's work exposes the ways in which such accumulation of information is represented (or misrepresented), and is enmeshed in cultural meanings written into the regulation of sexuality. This in turn helps us to make sense of important agendas in current health politics and to find strategies for confronting them.

Appropriation

The purpose and effect of those processes I have already discussed, *accommodation* and *accumulation*, is the *appropriation* of power. This refers to the containment and codification of 'scholarship' and 'knowledge' within dominating frameworks. Bhavnani (1991), Mohanty (1991), Opie (1992) and Said (1978, 1989), all explore the notion of appropriation, and offer a number of dimensions of it.

Said (1989) defines appropriation as the means by which the experiences of the 'colonized' are interpreted by a (more) dominant group to sustain a particular view of the 'other' as part of an ideological stance.

Opie (1992) quotes Clifford (1986) who identifies the appropriation of power in anthropological and ethnographic studies, which he criticises as disguising their inherent limitations. An example is the use of observation to record and typify characteristic behaviour and cultural ceremonies. Another is the employment of 'powerful abstractions' which enable ethnographers to assert their possession of the 'heart' of a culture, lacking reflexivity and suggesting that true statements about another culture can be made.

Bhavnani (1991) raises questions about so-called 'empowering' research, and makes the point that 'giving a voice' to oppressed groups does not necessarily constitute empowerment, although the two are often conflated. She quotes research where for instance black residents are presented by the researcher as victims or problems, and where direct speech extracts are used to confer an added voice of authenticity. Yet it is the researchers who appropriate and maintain power by making choices as to which quotes are relevant and whose descriptions appear to paint an objective picture of reality. She suggests that the inclusion of heretofore silenced voices cannot be seen as forms of resistance or challenge to domination unless there is provided a simultaneous analysis of those who are potential hearers, and why they do not hear.

..it is not only inaccurate to provide such a limited picture but...the processes which led to the initial silencing and then the permission to speak remain unconsidered and hence uninterrogated... further, it is necessary to make explicit the political framework which underpins such an interrogation. (Bhavnani 1991, p146)

Both Bhavnani and Opie point to the instability of data, its inconsistency and contradictions, that 'messiness' which is usually omitted to make research reports hygienic and clean. They argue that this absence of reflexivity results in such 'problems' being written out, thus limiting any analysis of power between researched and researcher.

Mohanty (1991) is scathing of some western feminists who appropriate power by their representation of third world women, a representation which assumes implicitly the west as the primary referent in theory and praxis. They do this in Mohanty's view, in a number of ways.

First by the assumption of women as a singular monolithic subject, an already constituted and coherent group with identified interests and desires; second on a methodological level, the uncritical way 'proof' of universality and cross-cultural validity are provided; third by the construction of 'third world difference',

that stable, ahistorical something that apparently oppresses most if not all the women.. (p54).

It is in the production of this 'third world difference' that Mohanty identifies western feminists' appropriation and colonisation of the constituent complexities which characterize the lives of women in third world countries.

The outcome of such research is a view of the 'typical' third world woman as victim and universal dependent, who is characterised by her object status in the writings of western feminists. As a result research on 'the veil', on women in purdah, on female genital mutilation, women's work, etc. distorts and disguises the contradictions inherent in women's location within various structures, along with effective political action and opposition.

Mohanty locates the appropriating, colonizing move in the assumption of 'women as an oppressed group'. By contrasting the representations of third world women with western feminists' (implicit) self-representations in the same context,

> we see that western feminists have become the true 'subjects' of this counterhistory. Third world women on the other hand, never rise above the debilitating generality of their 'object' status. (p71).

Mohanty cites as one exception the work of Maria Mies (1982), whose mode of local, political analysis

> generates theoretical categories *from within* the situation and context being analyzed...and also suggests corresponding effective strategies for organising against the exploitation... (p65)

Opie (1992) argues that textual appropriation can be avoided, or at least reduced by highlighting difference and by allowing many (contradictory and disruptive) voices to speak within the text. In this way she attempts to avoid appropriation of the data to the researcher's interests. But this view of appropriation posits it as a methodological 'problem' to be overcome by adjusting one's techniques. It risks leaving uncovered the political interests that underlie the research effort, and is open to the objections Bhavnani raised about 'giving a voice'. What is needed is a careful, historically specific analysis responsive to complex discursive and material realities. A central feature of such analysis must be a recognition that the field of social research is a myriad of unstable and heterogeneous relations of power.

Conclusion

In this chapter I have tried to unpack some dimensions of 'empowerment' in the research process which have not been fully explored in the research literature. I have offered a very tentative conceptual framework for judging the empowering potential of research design and methodology, and identified common oppressive processes in certain kinds of research, some of which claims to be 'empowering'. The framework suggested may or may not be useful, but what is certain is the need for some such yardstick. Where discussions of empowerment are not grounded in a theory of power and in the wider nexus of political, economic and social power relationships, too easily concerns about social justice can be incorporated into existing beliefs and ideologies. The beneficiaries are more likely to be the research professionals than the research subjects.

References

Bhavnani, KK (1991), What's Power Got To Do With It? Empowerment and Social Research, in eds. I.Parker and J.Shotter *Deconstructing Social Psychology*, London, Routledge.

Clifford, J and Marcus, G (1986) *Writing Culture: The Poetics and Politics of Ethnography*, University of California Press.

Edsall, T (1984) *The New Politics of Inequality*, NY, WW Norton.

Foucault, M (1978) *The History of Sexuality*, NY, Pantheon.

Foucault, M (1980) *Power/Knowledge: Selected Interviews and Other Writings*, New York, Pantheon.

Hakim, C (1987) *Research Design*, Allen and Unwin.

Hall, R (1992) Bias Among African-Americans Regarding Skin Color: Implications for Social Work Practice, in *Research on Social Work Practice*, Vol.2, Number 4, October.

Mama, A (1989) *The Hidden Struggle*, London Race and Housing Research Unit.

Mies, M (1982) *The Lace Makers of Narsapur*, London: Zed Press.

Mohanty, CT (1991) Cartographies of Struggle:Third World Women and the Politics of Feminism, in eds. CT Mohanty, A Russo & L Torres, *Third World Women and the Politics of Feminism*, Indiana Univ. Press.

Mohanty, CT (1991a) Under Western Eyes: Feminist Scholarship and Colonial Discourses, in eds. CT Mohanty, A Russo & L Torres, op cit.

Mort, F (1987) *Dangerous Sexualities*, Routledge and Kegan Paul.

Opie, A (1992) Qualitative Research, Appropriation of the Other and Empowerment, in *Feminist Review*, No.40, Spring 1992:52-69.

Said, EW (1978) *Orientalism*, Penguin.

Said,EW (1989) Representing the colonised:anthropology's interlocutors, in *Critical Inquiry* Vol.15:205-25.

Sawicki, J (1991) *Disciplining Foucault*, Routledge.

Sivanandan, A (1990) All that melts into the air is solid: the hokum of New Times, in *Race and Class*, Vol.31, No.3.

Smith, D (1987) *The Everyday World as Problematic: A Feminist Sociology*, Boston: Northeastern University Press.

Soper, K (1991) Postmodernism and its Discontents, in *Feminist Review* No.39: 97-114

Index

C

care, 16, 17, 38, 39, 40, 41, 42, 43,
44, 46, 47, 48, 49, 50, 51,.61, 62,
63, 64, 65, 68, 76, 77, 78, 103,
127, 149, 157, 169, 177, 178, 196
carers, 67, 68, 77, 78, 146, 170
case
files, 38, 45, 46, 47, 48
histories, 69
management, 68
categorisation, 4, 5, 92
censorship, 13, 85, 86
census, 43, 47, 48, 88
change, 1, 2, 6, 12, 14, 17, 27, 32,
63, 78, 104, 109, 110, 117, 141,
146, 147, 148, 149, 153, 154, 155,
157, 158, 159, 160, 161, 164, 165,
167, 174, 180, 187, 197, 198
characteristics, 3, 4, 14, 15, 22, 28,
51, 52, 61, 66, 90, 91, 124, 126,
173, 187
child development, 112
Children Act, 169, 177
choices, 31, 71, 72, 158, 201
class, 1, 3, 9, 22, 25, 26, 28, 30, 40,
51, 54, 83, 91, 94, 102, 103, 104,
106, 107, 141, 169, 173, 174, 186,
187, 188, 189, 195, 199
classification, 3, 5, 7, 92, 175, 199
coding, 74
cohort, 41, 43, 44, 47, 48, 50
collaborative forum, 150
colonialising
colonialism, 38, 192, 197
communication, 59, 60, 65, 71, 75,
77, 91, 141, 143, 158, 159, 187
community, 29, 30, 32, 33, 60, 61,
64, 68, 76, 78, 83, 86, 88, 89, 123,
125, 127, 128, 129, 130, 132, 134,
135, 136, 137, 139, 158, 179, 195
comparative, 43, 44, 64, 110
concepts, 3, 6, 13, 26, 66, 76, 78, 97,
109, 130, 186, 192
conceptual, 2, 3, 8, 12, 13, 21, 23,
47, 127, 186, 187, 197, 203
confidentiality, 53, 96
conflict, 39, 42, 77, 172, 194, 195

consent, 4, 61, 176
consultancy, 160
contextualising, 194
contradictions, 38, 187, 190, 194,
201, 202
control group, 68
counselling, 51, 59, 127, 128, 197
counterhegemonic, 104
Criminal Justice Act, 169
critical, 12, 13, 17, 103, 105, 107,
109, 112, 114, 117, 118, 119, 150
disclosure, 13
life history, 17, 105, 107, 109, 112,
114, 119
cultural invasion, 3, 140
culture, 25, 27, 28, 29, 40, 52, 160,
169, 172, 174, 188, 195, 196, 199,
200

D

data, 1, 4, 6, 7, 8, 12, 31, 44, 48, 49,
59, 61, 62, 63, 64, 66, 68, 69, 71,
72, 73, 76, 78, 79, 84, 88, 89, 90,
92, 95, 97, 124, 125, 129, 130,
132, 133, 136, 138, 156, 166, 175,
176, 179, 180, 193, 197, 201, 202
database, 64
deaf, 68, 78

decentralisation, 43
decision makers, 148
dependency, 62

development, 47, 67, 79, 109, 111,
  112, 114, 119, 124, 125, 126, 129,
  133, 137, 139, 146, 147, 149, 150,
  152, 153, 154, 155, 156, 157, 158,
  160, 186, 194
deviant, 13, 16, 75, 77, 97
diachronic, 111
dialogical, 105
dialogue, 3, 104, 108, 126, 140
difference, 1, 2, 15, 22, 25, 26, 27,
  28, 29, 30, 31, 32, 76, 91, 92, 93,
  104, 187, 188, 201, 202
Diploma in Social Work, 169
disability, 3, 6, 22, 25, 27, 28, 60,
  62, 63, 64, 68, 69, 79, 91, 102, 169
disabled, 3, 6, 26, 30, 68, 177, 179
discourse, 11, 15, 52, 126, 187, 188,
  198
disease, 15, 198, 199
documentary analysis, 45
documents, 38, 107, 108, 118, 119,
  132, 148, 179, 198, 199
dominated groups, 105, 114, 187,
  190
draw a man, 70
drawing, 6, 17, 32, 65, 66, 67, 70,
  72, 73, 74, 111, 118, 123, 156

___

E

education, 10, 32, 88, 103, 109, 125,
  131, 152, 169, 173, 192
empirical, 12, 23, 25, 37, 47, 50
employment, 82, 166, 174, 200

empowerment, 17, 123, 185, 186,
  187, 191, 197, 198, 201, 203
environment, 59, 76, 106, 112, 129,
  141, 143, 153
epistemological, 12, 21
equal opportunities, 14, 29, 45, 52,
  165, 166, 180
essentialism, 8, 176
ethics, 13, 14, 65, 104, 107, 117,
  118, 170
ethnic matching, 196
ethnic origin, ethnicity, 4, 22, 25, 37,
  38, 40, 46, 48, 49, 51, 54, 106,
  169, 174, 175, 176
Ethnograph, 71

ethnographic, 50, 63, 124, 126, 139,
  200
ethnography, 21, 37, 118

___

F

family
  as a social system, 110
  black, 39
  cycles, 109
  white nuclear, 52
fathers, 46
female, 91, 103, 112, 125, 166, 170,
  173, 174, 177, 185, 199, 202
feminist, feminists, 8, 10, 11, 12, 15,
  17, 21, 22, 23, 24, 25, 26, 27, 28,
  29, 30, 31, 32, 33, 85, 90, 91, 102,
  103, 104, 105, 106, 107, 108, 109,
  110, 111, 112, 123, 124, 125, 126,
  127, 128, 129, 142, 143, 186, 188,
  190, 201, 202
field study, 65
focused design, 71

oppression, oppressive,
anti-oppressive, 2, 8, 9, 15, 17, 89,
102, 103, 104, 105, 106, 110, 111,
112, 114, 117, 118, 123, 124, 126,
139, 165, 169, 185, 188, 190, 191,
194, 195, 197, 203
oral history, 102, 105, 106, 107
organisation,, 146, 150
Orientalism, 197, 198
outsider, 53, 54, 141

P

paradigm, 21, 23, 123, 124, 125,
127, 128
parent, 46, 52, 53, 158, 197
patriarchal structures, patriarchy, 9,
38
perception, 23, 66, 71, 76, 77, 107,
108, 113, 143
phenomenological perspective, 50
physically handicapped, 46
pilot study, 48
placement, 46, 49, 68, 82, 83, 96
policy, 4, 28, 31, 38, 77, 89, 90, 155,
165, 167, 170, 175, 180, 181
political, 1, 2, 3, 4, 7, 8, 9, 10, 11,
12, 14, 21, 23, 28, 32, 90, 93, 104,
106, 107, 111, 114, 117, 127, 141,
142, 160, 176, 185, 189, 192, 195,
197, 198, 199, 200, 201, 202, 203
politically incorrect, 51
politics
of black communities, 192, 194
populations, 47, 70, 112
positivist approach, 63, 64, 96
postmodernism, 187
poststructuralist, 9

power, 3, 9, 11, 12, 13, 14, 15, 26,
28, 31, 32, 37, 38, 41, 44, 45, 54,
77, 97, 104, 106, 109, 110, 111,
118, 125, 128, 132, 137, 142, 150,
167, 169, 177, 178, 185, 186, 187,
189, 190, 192, 194, 196, 197, 198,
199, 200, 201, 203
practice principles, 169
practitioner
research, 164, 165, 167, 169, 170,
172, 173, 174, 177, 180, 181
praxis, 27, 31, 201
probation, 17, 166, 170, 173, 176
psychology, 10, 87, 102, 103, 104,
111, 112, 113, 114, 118

Q

qualitative
investigation, 108
methods, 31, 132
quantitative
methods, 31, 45
questionnaires
mailed, 132, 133, 135
questions
chain of, 74
depth, 69, 72, 73
key, 70, 71, 178
structured, 65

R

race, 3, 4, 22, 25, 27, 28, 38, 39, 40,
46, 49, 51, 52, 54, 91, 102, 104,
169, 175, 176
Race Relations Act, 167
racism, 3, 4, 15, 37, 38, 51, 85, 86,
117, 166, 169, 172, 174, 176, 195
racist remarks, 52

service
  planning mechanisms, 149
  purchasers, 177, 178
  users, 38, 40, 59, 60, 61, 62, 103,
    146, 156, 157, 158, 161, 169,
    170, 175, 176, 177, 178, 179
sex similarities, differences, 49
sexism, 23, 38, 85, 174
sexual orientation, 169, 174
sexuality, 17, 22, 25, 28, 31, 85, 87,
  89, 90, 92, 94, 95, 102, 104, 127,
  189, 190, 199, 200
single mothers, 78
social
  divisions, 1, 27, 102, 104, 105,
    107, 108, 109, 110, 111, 114,
    117, 118
  justice, 126, 186, 187, 203
  medicine, 198
  networks, 110, 127
  research, 1, 2, 3, 4, 5, 6, 15, 16,
    21, 22, 24, 27, 32, 82, 84, 97,
    102, 103, 105, 106, 107, 110,
    111, 114, 118, 164, 173, 177,
    181, 187, 202
  services, 5, 10, 39, 40, 44, 53, 54,
    152, 165, 170
  structure, 107, 108, 118, 197
  systems, 108
social work
  research managers, 167
socialism, 187
sociological
  imagination, 104
space, ownership of, 77
speech, 51, 67, 72, 73, 77, 201
sphere, public and private, 11, 110
SPSSx, 71
stakeholder group, 158, 159

state bureaucracies, 195
statements test, 66, 70
statistical information, 43
statistics, 4, 31, 39
status, 5, 8, 46, 68, 78, 91, 94, 141,
  191, 202
steering group, 164, 170, 172, 174,
  175, 177, 178, 179, 180, 181
subject, 47, 71, 74, 93, 107, 108,
  114, 151, 167, 170, 173, 188, 196,
  201
subjective, 67, 69, 83, 107, 108, 113,
  119, 124
surveys, 5, 31, 60, 85, 86, 88, 89, 90,
  178, 193
symbol board, 73
symbolic interactionist, 64, 107
synchronic, 111
systemic, 110

T

tension release, 70
theoretical framework, 66, 105, 129,
  133, 195
theory, 24, 26, 27, 30, 37, 90, 103,
  112, 125, 127, 129, 143, 181, 185,
  186, 187, 194, 196, 201, 203
time
  family, 109
  historical, 109
  individual, 109
topic, single, 74
transcribable, transcribed,
  transcription, 64, 65, 67, 71, 74
transitions
  family, 110
  individual, 117
triangulate, triangulation, 97, 119

truth, 51, 83, 90, 93, 97, 156
Turkish Cypriot, 49, 51
twenty statements test, 66

U

unemployment, 7, 10, 11, 110, 165

V

validity, 43, 48, 65, 66, 67, 68, 71,
  77, 97, 108, 112, 113, 119, 123,
  201
  double, 113
  limitations of, 68
  of responses, 65
value free, 90
values, 13, 14, 66, 76, 79, 102, 103,
  104, 105, 106, 114, 117, 140, 146,
  186, 188
variable, 72
verbal skills, 69
violence, 16, 23, 78, 195, 196, 197
visual perception, 71
voice, giving a, 201, 202

W

war, 110, 188
West African, 49, 51
white, 3, 13, 15, 16, 25, 26, 30, 31,
  32, 49, 51, 52, 83, 91, 95, 103,
  112, 117, 164, 166, 167, 170, 172,
  173, 174, 176, 177, 178, 187, 192,
  195
White Indigenous, 49
women
  group, 130, 173, 179
  third world, 126, 190, 201, 202
  working class, 107, 195

Womens Health Centre, 130
Womens Studies, 22, 27
workers, exploitation of, 188
workshops
  pilot, 152
writing, 32, 52, 67, 73, 94, 113, 155,
  166, 177

Y

youth, 166, 172